GOD HAS A PLAN FOR

OUR NATION

CIVIL GOVERNMENT

For I know the plans I have for you," declares the LORD, "plans to prosper you and not to harm you, plans to give you hope and a future.
Jeremiah 29:11

By David Lange

GOD HAS A PLAN FOR OUR NATION
CIVIL GOVERNMENT
By David E. Lange

Copyright © 2014 David E. Lange

All rights reserved. No portion of this book may be reproduced, stored in a retrieval system, or transmitted in any form or by any means—electronic, mechanical, photocopy, recording, scanning, or other—except for brief quotations in critical reviews or articles, without the prior written permission of the publisher.

Unless otherwise indicated, Scripture quotations are taken from the HOLY BIBLE: NEW INTERNATIONAL VERSION®. © 1973, 1978, 1984 International Bible Society. Used by permission of Zondervan. All rights reserved.

Scripture quotations marked NLT are taken from the *Holy Bible,* New Living Translation, copyright 1996, 2004. Used by permission of Tyndale House Publishers, Inc., Wheaton, Illinois 60189. All rights reserved.

Published by Lange Publishing, Pacific, MO
Library of Congress Control Number: 2014911676
ISBN 978-0-9824070-5-9
ISBN 0-9824070-5-x
Printed in the United States of America

This book is dedicated to . . .

Christy. She is my wonderful, supportive, and beautiful wife. Without the support of her and my awesome kids, Jeremiah, Bethany, Sofia, Bentley, and Blake this work would not have been possible.

Dad and Mom. I cherish the godly parents that I have been blessed with.

Mission Community Church. I also want to acknowledge and thank our church family for putting up with me during this process.

Debra. My very supportive sister, her family, Jon Marc, Nathan, Micah, and Natalie.

Of course the greatest honor and glory goes to Jesus Christ, my Lord and Savior!

For more information check out
WWW.BIBLEISTHEROCK.COM

If you were blessed by this series check out
WWW.FIVECOMMITMENTS.COM

CONTENTS

MUST READ INTRODUCTION	1
TEN CIVIL GOVERNMENT LIFE TRUTHS	9
CIVIL GOVERNMENT 1 **YOU SHALL HAVE NO OTHER gODS**	13
CIVIL GOVERNMENT 2 **YOU SHALL NOT COMMIT IDOLATRY**	35
CIVIL GOVERNMENT 3 **YOU SHALL NOT MISUSE GOD'S NAME**	54
CIVIL GOVERNMENT 4 **REMEMBER THE SABBATH DAY**	71
CIVIL GOVERNMENT 5 **HONOR YOUR FATHER AND MOTHER**	94
CIVIL GOVERNMENT 6 **YOU SHALL NOT MURDER**	116
CIVIL GOVERNMENT 7 **YOU SHALL NOT COMMIT ADULTERY**	136
CIVIL GOVERNMENT 8 **YOU SHALL NOT STEAL**	159
CIVIL GOVERNMENT 9 **YOU SHALL NOT LIE**	182
CIVIL GOVERNMENT 10 **YOU SHALL NOT COVET**	210

MUST READ INTRODUCTION: GOD HAS A PLAN

God loves you. He created you. He longs for you to get to know Him better and to walk in His ways. God's love includes a plan for you, your family, the church, and the nation. He fully describes His plan in the Bible.

God's Word warns us about consequences that will occur when a nation turns away from Him. How do you think America is doing? Are we better off today? Are we worse off? The evidence is clear. We are experiencing some of God's consequences right now.

CONSEQUENCES FOR TURNING AWAY FROM GOD AND HIS WORD

- Debt - Deuteronomy 28:44
- More natural disasters – Deuteronomy 28:22-24; 2 Chronicles 7:13
- Losing God's protection – Deuteronomy 28:25
- A far away nation whose language we do not understand will come against us - Deuteronomy 28:49-50

President Andrew Jackson said, **"The Bible is the rock on which our republic rests."** This was true when our nation began, but it is no longer true today.

Today we have removed prayer, the Ten Commandments, and the Bible from our schools. Our families no longer devote time to studying Scripture and to following God's truths and principles.

People believe the lie that the founders wanted a separation of church and state. This lie distorts the meaning of the first amendment. It claims that having God in our schools breaks this amendment. But if this was true, would the authors and founders of the first amendment have had the Bible as the main textbook in their public schools? For four centuries, American families have cherished the Bible. They have believed it to be the rock on which this republic should rest.

In 1647, the first law for public education in America was called, "The Old Deluder Satan Act." The law declared, *"It being one chief project of that old deluder, Satan, to keep men from the knowledge of the Scriptures, as in former time…* Satan's goal is to keep men from the Holy Scriptures because God's Word is what leads people to a saving faith in Christ. Teaching Christianity is the best safeguard for any nation. To remove the teachings of Christ and His Word is to destroy a nation.

Societies of men must be governed in one way or another. They can either be governed with a heavy hand from a civil government or they can be self-governed based upon the teachings of Christ.

Heavy-handed government cannot restrain the sinfulness of man. Christ and Christ alone can change the character of man.

The foundation of Christ and His Word is what keeps a nation free. Do you think our nation is better off after removing God from our public schools? Are we less greedy, violent, or depressed? Are we more financially stable? Are our families more unified and loving or more separated and torn apart? America is suffering because we have taken God out of our lives. We need to repent and accept His perfect plan today.

Our country doesn't have to be this way. We can change the direction of this nation if we repent. Our founders knew this. They stood up and made a declaration to the world that they believed in a Creator. They understood that God had given them unalienable rights to be free and to worship Him as they pleased.

Do you believe the same? Are you willing to stand up for what you believe? Are you willing to cherish the Bible and begin studying it to find out what God's plan is for you, your family, the church, and our nation?

The four books in this series cover God's four ordained institutions: Self-Government / Family Government / Church Government / Civil Government.

They describe ten Life Truths for each institution. Each chapter presents a different Life Truth; a foundation for returning to God and for putting Him and His Word first in your life. Make a commitment to memorize these Life Truths as you work through the chapters.

CONSENT OF THE GOVERNED – ONE FAMILY AT A TIME

Our republic is still based upon the consent of the people. We are a government of the people, by the people, and for the people. As you return to God, and begin fulfilling the purposes God has for you in each of these institutions, seek to recruit others. Pray for our nation. Reach out to others in the hope that God will open their eyes and see the importance of obeying Him.

GOALS TO PRAY FOR:

- Individuals and families to return to studying, memorizing, and obeying God's Word
- Public schools to make the Bible the main textbook again
- The Ten Commandments to be obeyed and taught in our nation

ENGAGE PEOPLE WITH QUESTIONS LIKE THESE:

- Do you know that God has a plan for you, your family, the church, and our nation?
- Do you think our nation is headed in the right direction?
- Do you think our nation is more violent? More greedy?
- Do you think it was a good idea that we removed God and the Ten Commandments from our schools?
- Do you know God's Word says there will be consequences if we turn away from Him? *(Debt, loss of His protection, attacks from a nation from far away whose language we do not understand, more natural disasters)*
- Do you know that God will bless us if we turn back to Him?

FOLLOW UP WITH THIS QUESTION:

- Would you be interested in a Bible Study to learn more about God's plan for you, your family, the church, and our nation?

God allows suffering when we choose to turn away from Him. God promises blessings when we return to Him. Let's return to God and encourage everyone to do the same.

A PLAN OF ACTION FOR YOU, YOUR FAMILY, AND YOUR COMMUNITY:

1. Study and memorize the Life Truths for each institution.
2. Encourage others to join you (door to door, work, family, newspaper, etc…)
3. Encourage others to pray about running for a public office (school board, superintendent, alderman, mayor, etc…)
4. Begin a Facebook page or any other type of social media that will keep people informed (Have your goals clearly marked: We believe in God, the Apostles Creed, the Bible as the rock on which this nation rests, etc…) –This will help alert people to show up at City Hall for a vote or to voice their opinions.
5. Vote for Biblical laws. (Ex: a return to teaching the Bible in public schools)
6. **Direct people to the website *www.bibleistherock.com* for more information.**

A CHALLENGE FOR TODAY

Our founders understood the importance of knowing and heeding God's Word for future posterity. They also understood that godly leaders would need to be trained in the Bible. The first schools in our nation made sure that students got a Biblical education so they could lead with God's Word being the source for all law.

If we are going to have godly laws that lead us in righteousness, then we are going to need men and women who are willing to be the lawmakers. Who do we want in office making the laws that govern our nation? **Men and women who are God-fearing and who know the Bible well.**

For this to happen, "Christian" schools must make it a priority in their curriculum to raise up such leaders and prepare them for public offices. Not only do our "Christian" schools need to step up and refocus some of their goals, but we as a people need to engage more on a local level. We need to be willing to serve as mayors, aldermen, superintendents, and local school board members.

We must return to God so that He can forgive our sin and heal our land. We need to have a confidence and boldness to speak up for what we believe in. We need to study God's Word and teach all who will listen.

If we pray, study God's Word, obey Him, and spread the gospel, then we will be blessed by Him. God will hear our prayers, forgive our sins, and heal America again.

This is not an exhaustive study on the institutions just a starter guide to help us get things back into God's perfect order. *"His will being done on earth as it is in heaven."*

Read all four books and learn God's plan for the institutions.

Book 1 *God has a plan for you*
Self-Government

Book 2 *God has a plan for your family*
Family Government

Book 3 *God has a plan for the church*
Church Government

Book 4 *God has a plan for our nation*
Civil Government

May God bless you and may God bless our nation!

TEN CIVIL GOVERNMENT LIFE TRUTHS

1. YOU SHALL HAVE NO OTHER gODS BEFORE ME

Question: What does it mean to have no other gods before Him?
Answer: We must love God first; with all our heart, with all our soul, and with all our strength.

Exodus 20:1-3 (NIV) [1] And God spoke all these words: [2] "I am the LORD your God, who brought you out of Egypt, out of the land of slavery. [3] "You shall have no other gods before me.

2. YOU SHALL NOT COMMIT IDOLATRY

Question: What does it mean to commit idolatry?

Answer: Idolatry is when our devotion or allegiance goes towards anything other than God.

Exodus 20:4-6 (NIV) [4] "You shall not make for yourself an idol in the form of anything in heaven above or on the earth beneath or in the waters below. [5] You shall not bow down to them or worship them; for I, the LORD your God, am a jealous God, punishing the children for the sin of the fathers to the third and fourth generation of those who hate me, [6] but showing love to a thousand [generations] of those who love me and keep my commandments.

3. YOU SHALL NOT MISUSE THE NAME OF THE LORD

Question: What does it mean to misuse God's name?
Answer: We can misuse God's name in our speech, in our actions, and when we forget about its power.

Exodus 20:7 (NIV) [7] "You shall not misuse the name of the LORD your God, for the LORD will not hold anyone guiltless who misuses his name.

4. REMEMBER THE SABBATH DAY BY KEEPING IT HOLY

Question: What does it mean to keep the Sabbath holy? **Answer:** We are to keep the day holy by not doing any work or causing others to work.

Exodus 20:8-11 (NIV) [8] "Remember the Sabbath day by keeping it holy. [9] Six days you shall labor and do all your work, [10] but the seventh day is a Sabbath to the LORD your God. On it you shall not do any work, neither you, nor your son or daughter, nor your manservant or maidservant, nor your animals, nor the alien within your gates. [11] For in six days the LORD made the heavens and the earth, the sea, and all that is in them, but he rested on the seventh day. Therefore the LORD blessed the Sabbath day and made it holy.

5. HONOR YOUR FATHER AND MOTHER

Question: What does it mean to honor your father and mother?
Answer: Children are to learn how to respect God and others so that we can live long in the land.

Exodus 20:12 (NIV) [12] *"Honor your father and your mother, so that you may live long in the land the LORD your God is giving you.*

6. YOU SHALL NOT MURDER

Question: What does it mean to murder?
Answer: Murder is the unauthorized and intentional killing of a human life.

Exodus 20:13 (NIV) [13] *"You shall not murder.*

7. YOU SHALL NOT COMMIT ADULTERY

Question: What does it mean to commit adultery?
Answer: Adultery is the crime of unfaithfulness to your spouse.

Exodus 20:14 (NIV) [14] *"You shall not commit adultery.*

8. YOU SHALL NOT STEAL

Question: What does it mean to steal?
Answer: Stealing is a violation of a person's God given right to rule their own property.

Exodus 20:15 (NIV) ¹⁵ *"You shall not steal."*

9. YOU SHALL NOT LIE

Question: What does it mean to lie?
Answer: Lying is an intentional deception away from the truth.

Exodus 20:16 (NIV) ¹⁶ *"You shall not give false testimony against your neighbor.*

10. YOU SHALL NOT COVET

Question: What does it mean to covet?
Answer: Coveting is setting our hearts on earthly things instead of on heavenly things.

Exodus 20:17 (NIV) ¹⁷ *"You shall not covet your neighbor's house. You shall not covet your neighbor's wife, or his manservant or maidservant, his ox or donkey, or anything that belongs to your neighbor."*

CIVIL GOVERNMENT
LIFE TRUTH # 1
YOU SHALL HAVE NO OTHER gODS BEFORE ME

God has a plan for Civil Government. His plan includes prosperity, protection, liberty, and blessings. It is available to any nation that submits to His will. From Self Government to Civil Government, we are to govern our lives based upon His Word. Psalm 33:12 (NIV) [12] Blessed is the nation whose God is the LORD.

Patrick of Ireland was a missionary. He transformed the wicked and suffering nation of Ireland into a free and prosperous land. When he was about 15, he was captured in Britain and taken as a slave to Ireland. During his captivity, he turned to God and became a Christian. He prayed constantly and grew in his faith. He escaped around the age of 20, and was reunited with his family in Britain. But God compelled Patrick, in a dream, to return to Ireland and help the Irish people. He went to school and became a priest in the Catholic faith. The Catholic church commissioned him to be a missionary and to preach the gospel in Ireland.

When Patrick returned to Ireland, he started churches, met people's needs, and established local government. He wrote laws to help the people govern themselves. Patrick's main source in establishing the law was the Ten Commandments. Patrick knew that believing in the Gospel was a commitment to make Jesus the Lord of your life. Patrick transformed the nation with the Word of God. The people began to experience liberty and peace. The once pagan and oppressed nation became a peaceful land blessed by God.

Similarly, the founders of America established our nation based upon the Ten Commandments. As you read their writings, sixty percent of their quotes were from the Holy Bible, often including the Ten Commandments. The God of the Holy Scriptures was foundational in the establishment of America. William Federer says in his book <u>The Ten Commandments and their Influence on American Law</u>, pg. 54 "We have to look no further than our National Coinage, National Currency, National Motto, National Anthem, Pledge of Allegiance, Inaugural Addresses, State Constitutions, the wall above the chair of the Speaker of the House, National Monuments, National Day of Thanksgiving Proclamations, etc., to see examples."

America has been blessed because we established our Civil Government based upon the Ten Commandments and the teachings of Christ. The founders understood that our nation would collapse if we turned from the ways of God. John Adams stated in 1798, "Our Constitution was made only for a moral and religious people. It is wholly inadequate to the government of any other."

The founders understood and trusted in the Holy Scriptures as their source for wisdom. They based the foundation of this nation upon the Word of God. This is why we have printed on our money "In God We Trust." They also understood, that if we stopped governing ourselves based upon God's Word, our political system would collapse. This collapse is happening today. If our nation is going to be healed, we must repent, return to God's Word, and submit once again to His standards for our lives.

God promises blessings if we govern ourselves based upon His commands. Deuteronomy 28:1-2 (NIV) [1] If you fully obey the LORD your God and carefully follow all his commands I give you today, the LORD your God will set you high above all the nations on earth. [2] All these blessings will come upon you and accompany you if you obey the LORD your God:

God's law is like the law of gravity. If a person walks off a ten story building, they will fall to their death. You cannot get around the law of gravity. It is the same with the Ten Commandments and the teachings of Christ. You cannot get around God's Word. It is real and must be respected. If you respect and obey God's laws, things will go well with you. But if you reject His laws, there will be consequences.

Our nation is in a mess because we are no longer following the principles that were set out for us by our founding fathers. God's teachings have been gradually removed from our government and we are now experiencing the consequences.

Government is not a sinful word or a sinful position. It is a Biblical word and the position was instituted by God himself. God chose leaders. He gave them the laws by which to govern the people by. Abraham was chosen. Moses was chosen. Jesus even told Pilate that his position was given to him by God. John 19:11 (NIV) [11] Jesus answered, "You would have no power over me if it were not **given to you from above**. God puts people into positions of authority.
God not only places people in authority, but he gives people the spiritual gift of leadership, which allows them to govern in righteousness. Romans 12:6-8 (NIV) [6] We have different gifts, according to the grace given us. If a man's gift is prophesying, let him use it in proportion to his faith. [7] If it is serving, let him serve; if it is teaching, let him teach; [8] if it is encouraging, let him encourage; if it is contributing to the needs of others, let him give generously; **if it is leadership, let him govern diligently;** if it is showing mercy, let him do it cheerfully.

The Bible says in Romans 13:1-2 (NIV) [1] Everyone must submit himself to the governing authorities, for there is no authority except that which **God has established**. The authorities that exist **have been established by God**. [2] Consequently, he who rebels against the authority is rebelling against what **God has instituted**, and those who do so will bring judgment on themselves.

God expects people to obey the governing authorities. This passage lets us know that God is the one establishing people in office. It tells us that government is an institution created by God for the good of the people. God does not expect people to obey an authority that would lead them to disobey God's Word, but He does expect us to submit to the authorities that He has established.

What are the Biblical responsibilities of Civil Government? **This may surprise you, but the Civil Government is to be limited.** It is only to have a few responsibilities. The more that people govern themselves according to the Word of God, the less the civil government has to do. When nations turn away from the laws of God, their citizens begin to experience greater government oppression.

God must be firmly established in our first three institutions in order for us to establish His teachings in civil government. Each institution is a building block to a godly society. There is very little God in the government because there is very little God in our homes today. God must be in Self, Family, and Church Government before being manifested in our Civil Government. These building blocks are where we learn to love, obey, and fear God.

The Civil Government can be broken down into two main categories. The categories branch off into many different responsibilities, but are founded in these two God-ordained principles:

1. Establish the laws
2. Protect the Righteous

These two principles can be seen in this passage in Romans 13:1-5 (NIV) [1] Everyone must submit himself to the governing authorities, for there is no authority except that which God has established. The authorities that exist have been established by God. [2] Consequently, he who rebels against the authority is rebelling against what God has instituted, and those who do so will bring judgment on themselves. [3] For rulers hold no terror for those who do right, but for those who do wrong. Do you want to be free from fear of the one in authority? Then do what is right and he will commend you. [4] For he is God's servant to do you good. But if you do wrong, be afraid, for he does not bear the sword for nothing. He is God's servant, an agent of wrath to bring punishment on the wrongdoer. [5] Therefore, it is necessary to submit to the authorities, not only because of possible punishment but also because of conscience.

The governing authorities are to be God's servants. They are to seek God's Word in establishing and enforcing laws. A nation must understand that Jesus is Lord and humbly submit to His commands. Remember the prophecy about the baby Jesus in Isaiah 9:6-7 (NIV) [6] For to us a child is born, to us a son is given, and **the government will be on his**

shoulders. And he will be called Wonderful Counselor, Mighty God, Everlasting Father, Prince of Peace. [7] **Of the increase of his government and peace there will be no end.** He will reign on David's throne and over his kingdom, establishing and upholding it with justice and righteousness from that time on and forever. The zeal of the LORD Almighty will accomplish this.

There is no higher authority than God's throne. Everyone must submit to His law. However, because of our free will, we can make choices that do not honor Him. God is merciful and has great compassion, but He is also just. If we do not obey Him, we will suffer the consequences.

Jesus clearly stated that we will be blessed if we obey the commands of God. Matthew 5:17-19 (NIV) [17] "Do not think that I have come to abolish the Law or the Prophets; I have not come to abolish them but to fulfill them. [18] I tell you the truth, until heaven and earth disappear, not the smallest letter, not the least stroke of a pen, will by any means disappear from the Law until everything is accomplished. [19] Anyone who breaks one of the least of these commandments and teaches others to do the same will be called least in the kingdom of heaven, but whoever practices and teaches these commands will be called great in the kingdom of heaven.

Our founders depended on the Word of God to write the Constitution and government law. They made things legal and illegal based upon the standards of God's Word. They used the Ten Commandments and the teachings of Christ for their divine direction. On Feb.15, 1950, at the Attorney General's conference, Harry S. Truman said, "The fundamental basis of this nation's laws was given to Moses on the Mount." He was referring to the Ten Commandments. These laws were given to Moses on the mountain by God himself; written with His own hand. They were for all people and all nations. Nations that choose to submit to God, obey the Ten Commandments, and follow Christ's teachings are promised to experience blessings.

The Civil Government has a great responsibility in establishing our laws. This nation will stand before God one day and answer to Him for the laws they have established.

The second category is the protection of the righteous. A passage that reveals this truth is in I Peter 2:13-14 (NIV) [13] Submit yourselves for the Lord's sake to every authority instituted among men: whether to the king, as the supreme authority, [14] or to governors, who are sent by him to punish those who do wrong and to commend those who do right.

The government is to protect the righteous. It is to punish the evil doers and commend those who do right. To protect the righteous, the government may need to build prisons, establish military, and enter other countries to free oppressed people. These are aspects of a Biblical government.

The government is not supposed to establish healthcare, develop welfare systems, provide aid for disaster victims, or run a division of family services. These responsibilities have been placed, by God, in the jurisdiction of family and church government. These services were originally governed by the right institution in this nation. The sad truth, however, is that somewhere along the way things changed. Churches and families stopped governing themselves according to the Word of God. Consequently, government stepped in to help.

The debt we face today is just one of the outcomes of a government managing issues that are not part of God's plan. It takes money to handle most issues. Taxes go up. Debt increases. By not staying in God's designated jurisdictions we have allowed the government to do our work. Our nation is now experiencing God's judgment for governing outside of His divine order.

I asked Stephen McDowell, a historian, how to return to God's plan in the institutions? He said, "It will take a revival to return to God's plan. It will also be done gradually as we repent."

As Christians, we must do our part in the repentance of this nation. We must get our own lives in order. We must take care of family members who are struggling. We must also, as God provides, take care of the needy in our communities. Patrick of Ireland gave everything he had to return a nation to God and His commands. We should have the same kind of passion for Christ as he did. We are commanded to disciple the people around us and minister to their needs.

Our public schools used to teach the importance of the Ten Commandments to our children. Today, many churchgoers cannot even list all ten. As we continue studying our Civil Government Life Truths, we will be memorizing the Ten Commandments. We will also look deeper into their meaning and value for our lives.

The law is not only something that blesses our lives; it is also a schoolmaster designed to lead us to Christ. Galatians 3:24 (NIV) [24] So the law was put in charge to lead us to Christ that we might be justified by faith. As we study the law of God, we quickly realize that we have broken God's law and are in need of salvation. This is why Christ took the punishment that we deserve. In Christ's kingdom, as in His design for government, the evil doer must be punished. Christ took on the punishment that we deserve and continues to offer forgiveness and salvation to those who make Him their Lord. Through Christ, we are given the ability to turn away from our sinful selves and obey the law. Romans 8:4 (NIV) [4] in order that the righteous requirements of the law might be fully met in us, who do not live according to the sinful nature but according to the Spirit.

A nation that does not follow Christ and His teachings becomes more and more corrupt. By **removing Christ from our educational system, we remove the only ability there is for self-restraint and godly living.** Without Christ and His laws, we are left to our own opinions for morality. Corruption in our current generation is the result of legalizing things that are identified as sin according to God's Word.

The first commandment is in Exodus 20:3 (NIV)
[3] "You shall have no other gods before me."
Let's say that you are an inventor who built a marvelous machine that could bless many people. How would you feel if everyone ignored you and gave you no credit? How would you feel if everyone used your machine and benefited from it, but no one thanked you? Let's say that your machine could even perform miracles. Would it bother you that many were using it and being blessed by it without any signs of gratitude or appreciation? This is how God must feel, as his creation breathes His air, walks on His land, lives on His property, and eats the food that He grows, without a thank you.

The term god means Supreme Being. There is none other than the Almighty God. Throughout Scripture the Bible declares that there is no other God. Joel 2:27 (NIV) [27] Then you will know that I am in Israel, that I am the LORD your God, and that there is no other;

In declaring the first command, God is telling us that our devotion needs to be solely towards Him and no other. We cannot worship the sun, food, stars, or anything else that He has created. We must worship the one who created it all and gave it to us for our pleasure. We should not make up false gods and worship them. This is breaking the first commandment.

In our generation, we are being told that all religions worship the same god. This contradicts Scripture. The Scriptures declare that there is only one God. All other gods must not be worshiped or given devotion of any kind. To say that Islam, Buddha, Hinduism, Mormons, and Jehovah Witnesses all worship the same god is false. To accept these religions as equal is to bring other gods up to the level of God himself. These religions deny that Jesus is God. The command states that we are not to bring any other god's into or equal with His position. He is God Almighty alone. There is no other.

The Bible declares that Jesus is God. Scriptures tell us that God is the Father, the Son, and the Holy Spirit. These three persons are the one Almighty God. Deuteronomy 6:4-5 (NIV) [4] Hear, O Israel: The LORD our God, the LORD is one. [5] Love the LORD your God with all your heart and with all your soul and with all your strength.

Our generation has twisted the words separation of church and state into something that the founders of this nation never meant them to be. The founding fathers penned these words to hopefully prevent a Christian denomination from ever gaining total control again. The Church of England had dictated everything from their taxes to how they would worship God. They wanted to make sure their new freedom, to worship the Judeo Christian God spoken of in the Scriptures, was protected by law. The founders never meant for this nation to accept all religions as equal and keep God out of government. The command to have no other gods goes much deeper than just the false gods that people in every generation have chosen to worship. It goes deep into our hearts, revealing what we love the most. **God demands that we love Him more than anything!** The truth is that we are all guilty of breaking this command. We are foolish people who sometimes worship created things instead of the Creator.

Paul talks about the "god" that takes away the worship that only God deserves. Philippians 3:19 (NIV) [19] Their destiny is destruction, **their god** is their stomach, and their glory is in their shame. Their mind is on earthly things. The symbolic phrase "their god is their stomach" is referring to our devotion to things and our passion for things. Things that please our flesh can many times get our devotion and we forget that our love and devotion is solely for the Almighty.

We can eat a delicious meal and savor every bite, but our heart issue is what we worship. Do we worship the food that gives us pleasure? David says in 1 Chronicles 16:8-12 (NIV) **8** Give thanks to the LORD, call on his name; make known among the nations what he has done. **9** Sing to him, sing praise to him; tell of all his wonderful acts. **10** Glory in his holy name; let the hearts of those who seek the LORD rejoice. **11** Look to the LORD and his strength; seek his face always.

God is our provider, sustainer, and protector. Jesus taught us that this command is the greatest command of them all. Matthew 22:37-38 (NIV) **37** Jesus replied: "'Love the Lord your God with all your heart and with all your soul and with all your mind.' **38** This is the first and greatest commandment.

This is the first of the Ten Commandments and the greatest of them all. It is also the most difficult to keep as humans. We love to be self-sufficient and strive to have everything under control. We pursue what pleases us and makes us happy. Many times our pursuit of happiness leads to our own suffering and the suffering of others. When we keep our devotion to God in its proper place, we save ourselves from unnecessary pain and suffering.

God created us to be free and to make our own decisions. However, decisions that go against His will for our lives, destroy us, and lead us down a road of destruction and pain. **To pursue what you want**

instead of pursuing what God desires for you is sin! This is making yourself a god and your desires more important than His.
When a nation disobeys God's laws, He allows leaders to rise up and drive the people into slavery and oppression. God's intent, in this state, is for the people to cry out to Him and ask Him for help. Tyranny is a consequence of not loving God more than anything. It is the law of God that must be respected or the consequences will fall. When our nation tries to tell us to be tolerant, and accept all religions as believing in the same god, we must realize that this is like walking off a ten story building. We cannot change the laws of God. They are written in stone. They will either bless us or curse us.

How do we know if our devotion is in the right place?

1. Obedience

Jesus revealed the answer to us in John 14:15 (NIV) [15] "If you love me, **you will obey what I command**. John expresses this measuring stick as well in 1 John 2:3 (NIV) [3] We know that we have come to know him **if we obey his commands**. 1 John 5:3 (NIV) [3] **This is love for God: to obey his commands**. And his commands are not burdensome.

Our devotion to the one true God is evident in our obedience to Him. If we say that we love God, yet we do sinful things, we can be assured the god of our life is not Jesus. When we are obeying the command to have no other gods, the god of self must be removed as well. When we live for sexual immorality, greed, food, drugs, pleasures, or fame, we are seeking to please the god of self, not the God of the universe.

2. Praise

We learned in Self Government that praise toward God is one of the main reasons we have been created. Praise is evident in our actions, but also in our hearts. What are we thankful for? Where do our accolades go?

"Father, I thank you for today." "I thank you for all that I have and all that I am." We fall short in lifting our voices to the Lord in praise for all He has done and is going to do for us. We must discipline ourselves to be devoted to God; giving Him all the praise that He deserves.

Praise is like a barometer of your love for God. We do not want to praise if we are living in disobedience to His commands. We do not want to praise if we are focusing on our wants instead of pursuing His plan for our lives. Romans 15:11 (NIV) [11] And again, "Praise the Lord, all you Gentiles, and sing praises to him, all you peoples."

3. Relationship

How does your spouse or family know that you love them? Do you send them a check and say "Hi" to them once a week? Are your conversations short and without feeling? Of course not. These are not the ways you show people you love that they are important to you. You show them that you love them with quality time. You listen to their thoughts, feelings, and emotions. You pray for them. You seek to meet their needs. You bless them. You look for ways to make them happy. You give them gifts to see them smile.

Did you know that if we do these kinds of actions for our family, but neglect doing the same things for God, we are sinning? Loving our family can get in the way of our devotion to God. We must love God first. It must be with all our heart, with all our mind, and with all our strength. To do anything else is to bring another god before him.

Look at what Jesus said in Matthew 10:37-38 (NIV)
[37] "Anyone who loves his father or mother more than me is not worthy of me; anyone who loves his son or daughter more than me is not worthy of me; [38] and anyone who does not take his cross and follow me is not worthy of me.

Jesus is claiming deity in this passage. Our first devotion must be to God. We are to have no other gods before Him. We must love God more than anything. Nothing supersedes this first command. Jesus is God!

How do we grow in our relationship with Christ? We get to know Him by spending quality time with Him. We study His Word to find out what pleases Him. Just as we study our children to find out what pleases them, we study the Word to find out what pleases the Lord. In fact, we are to seek to please the Lord before we seek to please our children. Look at this passage in Ephesians 5:8-10 (NIV) [8] For you were once darkness, but now you are light in the Lord. Live as children of light [9] (for the fruit of the light consists in all goodness, righteousness and truth) [10] and find out what pleases the Lord.
If you are living in violation to His commands, then God is not first in your life. You have other gods before Him. God's Words says, "You shall have no other gods before Him."

Are there things that you are doing that would displease the Lord? Are you neglecting the time that you should be spending pursuing the Lord by pursuing other pleasures? Is His praise continually on your lips? Hebrews 13:15 (NIV) [15] **Through Jesus, therefore, let us continually offer to God a sacrifice of praise**--the fruit of lips that confess his name.

Do you know what pleases the Lord? Are you obeying Him to bring Him praise? Are you pursuing Him to get to know Him because you love Him?

Psalm 42:1-2 (NIV) [1] As the deer pants for streams of water, so my soul pants for you, O God. [2] My soul thirsts for God, for the living God. When can I go and meet with God?

If this is not your heart's passion and devotion, repent. Turn to God and cry out to Him for forgiveness and mercy. "Lord forgive me for loving the things of this world more than I love you. Help me, Lord, to have no other gods before you. Help me to love you with everything I have. Lord, I want to know you and the power of your resurrection. Fill me with your Spirit and guide me in the paths of righteousness, for your name's sake. In Jesus name I pray, Amen."

WORKSHEET FOR CIVIL GOVERNMENT
LIFE TRUTH # 1
YOU SHALL HAVE NO OTHER
gODS BEFORE ME

Question: What does it mean to have no other gods before Him?
Answer: We must love God first; with all our heart, with all our soul, and with all our strength.

Exodus 20:1-3 (NIV) [1] And **God spoke all these words**: [2] "I am the LORD your God, who brought you out of Egypt, out of the land of slavery. [3] You shall have no other gods before me."

> Write out the Life Truth, question, and answer on one side of an index card and the verse on the other side. Keep it in your Bible for the week. Work on it every day individually and as a family. Have it memorized by next week.

Read Deuteronomy 6:4-9. How many gods are there?

What does the passage say as to how we are to love God?

Do all religions believe in the same god?

What verse would you use to defend your answer?

Read Exodus 20:3. What do you think it means to have no other gods before me?

Read John 14:15-24. What will be evident if God is our first love?

The kind of god that a person believes in will determine their actions. Give a modern day example.

Is this statement true or false: To have no other gods means that we govern our lives by what God says for us to do according to His Words in the Bible.

Why is the first commandment important for businesses to adhere by?

What evidences have you seen in our generation of businesses who obeyed or disobeyed the command?

Why is the first commandment important for governments to adhere by?

What evidences have you seen in our generation of our government obeying or disobeying the command?

Nothing should come before our love for God. What kinds of things can distract us and cause us to put them before our love for God?

What are some evidences that will be displayed in our daily life if we love God first?

Read Psalm 95:6-7. Kneel in prayer, individually or as a family and recommit to making God first in your life. Ask Jesus to forgive you and then to enable you to obey the first commandment.

Based on this LIFE TRUTH what can you do individually and as a family to have no other gods before Him? How can you help others to obey this command?

CIVIL GOVERNMENT
LIFE TRUTH # 2
YOU SHALL NOT COMMIT IDOLATRY

The first commandment tells us that the object of our worship must be God and God alone. It is the second commandment that warns us about the mode of our worship. These two commandments are similar in that our devotion, worship, and allegiance must be to God and God alone.

The second commandment condemns any mode we use to worship that is not worshiping the one true God. The second commandment states in *Exodus 20:4-6 (NIV)* *⁴ "You shall not make for yourself an idol in the form of anything in heaven above or on the earth beneath or in the waters below. ⁵ You shall not bow down to them or worship them; for I, the LORD your God, am a jealous God, punishing the children for the sin of the fathers to the third and fourth generation of those who hate me, ⁶ but showing love to a thousand [generations] of those who love me and keep my commandments.*

God spoke these two verses just before He gave the people of Israel the Ten Commandments. *Exodus 20:1-2 (NIV) ¹ And God spoke all these words: ² "I am the LORD your God, who brought you out of Egypt, out of the land of slavery.* God is reminding the nation of Israel of His awesome power; that He is God; and there is no other. The Israelites were currently living in captivity among the Egyptians who worshiped idols. The Egyptians regularly called upon these false gods to bless them and make them prosper. For a time, it even seemed like their false gods were real because of how they were prospering.

During their captivity, the Israelites themselves began to engage in idol worship hoping to be blessed and possibly even freed from their bondage. We know this because of what they did when they were waiting for Moses to return from the mountain with the Ten Commandments. They made a golden calf and sought to worship it, hoping that they would be blessed and provided for. After all, they had witnessed this type of idol worship by the Egyptians.

The Bible is clear that the Israelites were not freed because of any idol. They were freed because their cries made it to the ears of the Almighty. *Exodus 2:23-25 (NIV) 23 During that long period, the king of Egypt died. The Israelites groaned in their slavery and cried out, and their cry for help because of their slavery went up to God. 24 God heard their groaning and he remembered his covenant with Abraham, with Isaac and with Jacob. 25 So God looked on the Israelites and was concerned about them.*

During the exodus of the nation of Israel, God placed a great many plagues upon the Egyptians, sparing the Israelites. He showed Himself to be the One True God, proving that their idolatry was worthless. God reminded the Israelites that He was the one who had freed them from slavery. "I am the LORD your God, who brought you out of Egypt, out of the land of slavery."

We are told not to make for ourselves an idol of any kind. This means idolatry is more than just worshiping a graven image. It is worshiping anything other than God. Our God is a jealous God. The Second Commandment gives us strict warnings on idolatry and the devastation it will cause to future generations.

What is an idol?

In the Old Testament, nations often made graven images and prayed to them for guidance, provisions, or protection. These forms of devotion were to be directed only to God. Idolatry was condemned by the prophets repeatedly in the Old Testament. Look at this passage in Ezekiel:

Ezekiel 8:9-18 (NIV) [9] And he said to me, "Go in and see the wicked and detestable things they are doing here." [10] So I went in and looked, and I saw portrayed all over the walls all kinds of crawling things and detestable animals and all the idols of the house of Israel. [11] In front of them stood seventy elders of the house of Israel, and Jaazaniah son of Shaphan was standing among them. Each had a censer in his hand, and a fragrant cloud of incense was rising. [12] He said to me, "Son of man, have you seen what the elders of the house of Israel are doing in the darkness, each at the shrine of his own idol? They say, 'The LORD does not see us; the LORD has forsaken the land.'"*¹³* Again, he said, "You will see them doing things that are even more detestable." *¹⁴* Then he brought me to the entrance to the north gate of the house of the LORD, and I saw women sitting there, mourning for Tammuz. *¹⁵* He said to me, "Do you see this, son of man? You will see things that are even more detestable than this." *¹⁶* He then brought me into the inner court of the house of the LORD, and there at the entrance to the temple, between the portico and the altar, were about twenty-five men. With their backs toward the temple of the LORD and their faces toward the east, they were bowing down to the sun in the east. *¹⁷* He said to me, "Have you seen this, son of man? Is it a trivial matter for the house of Judah to do the detestable things they are doing here? Must they also fill the land with violence and continually provoke me to anger? Look at them putting the branch to their nose! *¹⁸* Therefore I will deal with them in anger; I will not look on them with pity or spare them. Although they shout in my ears, I will not listen to them."*

Idolatry is a focus of devotion on the wrong object. The end result in idolatry may be a "good" thing but the devotion, worship, or allegiance is the focus. A woman may desire to have a baby, and in pursuit of this desire, seeks out a foreign god to bless her with a child. A man may desire to grow a crop to feed his family, and in pursuit of this desire, burns incense to a foreign god.

Idolatry, in the New Testament, becomes a matter of the heart. It no longer has to be the worship of a graven image; it can be a mindset, a philosophy, a practice, a value, a way of thinking, etc...

Paul warns Christians to flee from the passions of the flesh. He associates these earthly desires with idolatry. *Colossians 3:5 (NIV) [5] Put to death, therefore, whatever belongs to your earthly nature: sexual immorality, impurity, lust, evil desires and greed, which is idolatry.*

Our pursuits for evil desires are idolatrous to God. God alone demands and expects worship. When we pursue the pleasures of this world, over pursuing God, we commit idolatry. Do you desire sexual fulfillment more that you desire God? Do you desire money more than you desire God? Do you desire pleasure, comfort, or entertainment more than you desire God?

We have all broken this command, just as we have broken the command to have no others gods before him. The law makes it clear that we are sinners and in need of Christ. It is only through Christ that we can obey the law.

Most of our desires, when used in the right context, are blessings from God. But when we pursue these blessings, more than we are pursue God, we commit idolatry. For example, sexual fulfillment is a beautiful thing and a blessing from God. However, it is only for the marriage bed. To fulfill this passion outside of the will of God is idolatry. Provisions are wonderful things and are blessings from God. To worship provisions, forgetting that they come from God, is idolatry. Protection, comfort, and entertainment are all blessings from God. But if we pursue them, rather than the worship of God, they become curses.

A person can be consumed with the things of this world to the demise of their own life. Devotion and worship must be directed towards God. To neglect quality time with the Lord, in pursuit of one of His blessings, is to have a sinful mode of worship. Our first pursuit must be to know the Giver of all things and to be content in all circumstances. If God blesses us with more, then we praise Him for it. If He takes away, we still praise Him. Our devotion must remain focused on Him.

Philosophies, mindsets, and other ways of thinking can steal our devotion and cause us to neglect the ways of God. There is a *politically correct* philosophy gaining ground across America. Christians are afraid to speak up for fear that they may be labeled narrow-minded bigots. They are devoted to their comfort zone rather than to the will of God. This too is idolatry. Pursuing comfort and avoiding persecution is a mode of devotion over engaging society with the truth.

Mark 8:38 (NIV) *38 If anyone is ashamed of me **and my words** in this adulterous and sinful generation, the Son of Man will be ashamed of him when he comes in his Father's glory with the holy angels."*

We cannot be ashamed of Christ or His teachings. As followers, we need to be telling people the truth according to the Word of God.

There is a massive effort to control the thoughts of our children and to educate them into this new philosophy. God is not to be spoken about in our public schools. His Ten Commandments are not to be taught. How can we exist if our devotion, worship, and allegiance is not directed to our God? If we turn our backs on the God who created us, this life on earth is futile.

Allegiance to God and nothing else is the goal for our lives. Allegiance means that we will be faithful, devoted, and committed to the ways of God. If we believe that something is not sin, but God's Word tells us that it is sin, where should our allegiance go? If our allegiance goes to our own beliefs, we commit idolatry. When we trust in ourselves, our devotion turns away from God.

For example, God's Word tells us to get rid of our filthy language. Yet many believe that cursing is not sinful and is a choice we can make. *Colossians 3:8 (NIV)* [8] *But now you must rid yourselves of all such things as these: anger, rage, malice, slander, and filthy language from your lips.* Where will our allegiance go? Will we be faithful to God and His Word, knowing that He has the best in mind for us? Or will we be faithful to ourselves?

Worship is a human response to the perceived presence of God. God's presence is everywhere. We should be worshiping God everywhere and in everything. Worship is more than just meeting together on Sunday mornings. Every day should be filled with praise and worship to God. Everything we do, everything we say, and everything we think, needs to glorify to God.

Why does idolatry make God so jealous?
Idolatry makes God angry because it takes away from the worship that He deserves. It takes away from the devotion that is expected in covenantal relationships. If my wife came home and found a picture of another woman next to hers, what would she think? First, she would want to know *who* and *why* this woman's picture was next to hers. She would be furious if I told her that this woman was someone I had been spending time with and was seeking to know and to please. And rightly so! My devotion in marriage is to be solely for my wife and her alone.

God demands that our first love be towards Him and Him alone. This does not mean that we should not love our wives or our families. God commands us to love them as well. He enables us to love others more than we could ever do on our own. *Romans 5:5 (NIV) [5] And hope does not disappoint us, because God has poured out his love into our hearts by the Holy Spirit, whom he has given us.*
We are better at everything when we put God first in our lives. This nation has committed the idolatry

of allegiance. We are proud Americans. We puff out our chests and say how powerful we are. But this country should not be our first allegiance. Our first allegiance is to God. He wants us to be devoted citizens. But when we have an allegiance to country that surpasses an allegiance to God; it is idolatry. We are a great nation only because God made us great. If we turn away from the Ten Commandments and push God out of our schools and public buildings, we will see His punishments come upon us. The punishments will not only come upon us, but will also come upon our children to the third and fourth generations. *You shall not bow down to them or worship them; for I, the LORD your God, am a jealous God, punishing the children for the sin of the fathers to the third and fourth generation of those who hate me.* When we choose to worship anything other than God, it is a sign that we hate Him.

Haiti is one of the poorest nations in our generation. It experienced one of the most devastating earthquakes in history. It recently experienced a massive hurricane. Many of its people still suffer from diseases. Has Haiti always been one of the poorest nations? No. Haiti used to be under the control of France and was a prosperous nation. In 1791, the slaves in Haiti revolted and cried out in Voodoo worship. They sacrificed a pig to a false god and drank its blood. The slaves overcame their oppressors and gained freedom in 1804. Their idol worship continued. As a result, they have suffered great poverty, disease, and natural disasters for over

200 years. God longs to help them, as He does every nation, but first they must seek Him and keep His commandments.

America began as one nation under God. Our founding fathers were devoted to keeping God's commands and to putting Him first in all things. If we turn away from Him now, do we really understand the devastation that awaits us? People claim that we are an enlightened generation; exploring new levels of knowledge and understanding. If we continue to believe in ourselves by rejecting the one true God, we will suffer just like every other nation who has not put God first.

The blessings that we experience today in our nation are due to the men and women who have gone before us. They put God first in their lives and obeyed His commands.

Why are the consequences of idolatry passed down to other generations?

Idolatry is demon worship. It causes us to sin. Sin is powerful and will eventually enslave us. *Romans 6:5-7 (NIV) [5] If we have been united with him like this in his death, we will certainly also be united with him in his resurrection. [6] For we know that our old self was crucified with him so that the body of sin might be done away with, that we should no longer be slaves to sin– [7] because anyone who has died has been freed from sin.*

The phrase *the body of sin might be done away with* can also be translated rendered powerless. When we worship demons, they begin to destroy, divide, and enslave us. The consequences of idolatry worship will be felt for many generations. What will we leave to our future generations? Will they be experiencing blessings or curses?

The Bible speaks about the idolatry of the Israelites in *Deuteronomy 32:16-17 (NIV) [16] They made him jealous with their foreign gods and angered him with their detestable idols. [17] They sacrificed to demons, which are not God— gods they had not known, gods that recently appeared, gods your fathers did not fear.* Who were they sacrificing to? Demons! Idolatry opens the door to demons.

Idolatry may seem harmless and innocent at first, but it progresses into great evil. A nation may begin to worship a false god for provisions. The nation may be blessed and think that all is well. But as the provisions stop, new ways to worship false gods are developed. These demons influence people to do horrible things as written about in *Jeremiah 32:34-35 (NIV) [34] They set up their abominable idols in the house that bears my Name and defiled it. [35] They built high places for Baal in the Valley of Ben Hinnom to sacrifice their sons and daughters to Molech, though I never commanded, nor did it enter my mind, that they should do such a detestable thing and so make Judah sin.*

In our nation, many have embraced the philosophy that women should have equal rights. The devotion to this philosophy, allowing this belief to supersede the law of God, has now turned into a woman's right to kill her own baby. Many falsely believe that they are protecting women's rights; but they are no more than pawns, used by the devil, to destroy human life.

Many have embraced the unbiblical philosophy of tolerance in this nation. We are told that we must be tolerant of others beliefs. This tolerance has caused people to be intolerant of Christianity; even expecting children in elementary schools to sing songs in Aramaic. These Aramaic songs are actually praise songs to Allah. If God is God, and there is no other, don't you think it makes Him jealous that his little children are singing praise songs to a demon? Without Christ in our schools, we have lost the ability to publicly train our children the only way to live upright and godly lives.

Many people know this passage in 1 Corinthians, Chapter 10, verse 13, "*[13] No temptation has seized you except what is common to man. And God is faithful; he will not let you be tempted beyond what you can bear. But when you are tempted, he will also provide a way out so that you can stand up under it."* Notice how the context of this passage refers to idolatry:

1 Corinthians 10:1-22 (NIV) [6] Now these things occurred as examples to keep us from **setting our hearts on**

evil things as they did. Idolatry is setting our hearts on something other than God.

This passage reminds us of certain events in history and calls the people who committed these sins idolaters. *⁷ **Do not be idolaters,** **as some of them were**; as it is written: "The people sat down to eat and drink and got up to indulge in pagan revelry." ⁸ We should not commit sexual immorality, as some of them did—and in one day twenty-three thousand of them died. ⁹ We should not test the Lord, as some of them did—and were killed by snakes. ¹⁰ And do not grumble, as some of them did—and were killed by the destroying angel.*
¹¹ These things happened to them as examples and were written down as warnings for us, on whom the fulfillment of the ages has come.

We are all tempted to set our hearts on things that go against the will of God for our lives. These people were probably thinking that they were headed in the right direction. Do you think that any of them understood that they were about to drive right off a bridge and into hell? God's Word gives us the road signs to keep us from driving off a bridge to our own destruction. The Ten Commandments are our road signs. We must keep our hearts away from evil things.

The passage goes on to tell us *¹² So, if you think you are standing firm, be careful that you don't fall! ¹³ No temptation has seized you except what is common to man. And God is faithful; he will not let you be tempted*

beyond what you can bear. But when you are tempted, he will also provide a way out so that you can stand up under it. God promises to provide a way out for us. We do not have to succumb to our temptations.
14 Therefore, my dear friends, flee from idolatry. Flee from your evil desires and seek the Lord. Place your devotion in Him alone.

Paul goes on to remind us that committing idolatry is worshiping demons, **15** I speak to sensible people; judge for yourselves what I say. **16** Is not the cup of thanksgiving for which we give thanks a participation in the blood of Christ? And is not the bread that we break a participation in the body of Christ? **17** Because there is one loaf, we, who are many, are one body, for we all partake of the one loaf. **18** Consider the people of Israel: Do not those who eat the sacrifices participate in the altar? **19** Do I mean then that a sacrifice offered to an idol is anything, or that an idol is anything? **20** No, but **the sacrifices of pagans are offered to demons, not to God, and I do not want you to be participants with demons.** **21** You cannot drink the cup of the Lord and the cup of demons too; you cannot have a part in both the Lord's table and the table of demons. **22** Are we trying to arouse the Lord's jealousy? Are we stronger than he?

This passage, as well as the one in Deuteronomy, associates idolatry with the worship of demons. Idolatry is succumbing to evil desires; putting them before our devotion and allegiance to God. In doing this, we become devoted to pleasures more than to

God. We offer our worship to demons rather than to God.

God set His people free from the Egyptians so they could worship Him. *Exodus 8:1 (NIV)* [1] *Then the LORD said to Moses, "Go to Pharaoh and say to him, 'This is what the LORD says: Let my people go, so **that they may worship me**.*

When we are devoted to anything more than we are devoted to God, we are committing idolatry. Those who worship themselves, devoted to their own beliefs and opinions, are really worshiping Satan. People are not in control of their own destiny. They either worship God or worship the devil.

Satan wants us to worship things. He wants us to give our allegiance and devotion to acquiring the things of this earth. He wants us to set our hearts on earthly things rather than on God. God wants to bless us. He wants us to ask Him for our blessings. But we must never want anything more than we want God.

The Bible says in *Revelation 13:8 (NIV)* [8] *All inhabitants of the earth will worship the beast—all whose names have not been written in the book of life belonging to the Lamb that was slain from the creation of the world.*

People don't say to themselves, "Let's go worship the devil." Satan tricks people. He influences them into chasing after their wants rather than chasing after God.

The promise in the second command is that God will bless and show love to *a thousand [generations] of those who love me and keep my commandments*. Will we be the ones who put our allegiance to Christ and Christ alone? Will we keep His commandments and the Words written in His Holy Word?

From angels to humans, every creation of God is to keep His commands and worship Him. At the end of the book of Revelation, John is about to fall down and worship the angel that has revealed future events, but the angel stops him. *Revelation 22:8-9 (NIV) [8] I, John, am the one who heard and saw these things. And when I had heard and seen them, I fell down to worship at the feet of the angel who had been showing them to me. [9] But he said to me, "Do not do it! I am a fellow servant with you and with your brothers the prophets and of all who keep the words of this book. Worship God!"*

WORKSHEET FOR CIVIL GOVERNMENT
LIFE TRUTH # 2
YOU SHALL NOT COMMIT IDOLATRY

Question: What does it mean to commit idolatry?
Answer: Idolatry is when our allegiance or worship goes towards anything other than God.

Exodus 20:4-6 (NIV) ⁴ "You shall not make for yourself an idol in the form of anything in heaven above or on the earth beneath or in the waters below. ⁵ You shall not bow down to them or worship them; for I, the LORD your God, am a jealous God, punishing the children for the sin of the fathers to the third and fourth generation of those who hate me, ⁶ but showing love to a thousand [generations] of those who love me and keep my commandments.

> Write out the Life Truth, question, and answer on one side of an index card and the verse on the other side. Keep it in your Bible for the week. Work on it every day individually and as a family. Have it memorized by next week.

Read Exodus 32. Why did the people make an idol?

Why do you think God asked the people to kill their own family members?

What was the consequence for their sin?

Did it come immediately after they sinned?

In the command to not make any idols, God says He is a jealous God. What is God jealous of?

Read Colossians 3:5 What two things are considered idolatry in this passage?

Give an example of something that could be idolatry today?

Circle the words that can become idols to us: (work, entertainment, comfort, money, relationships, security, religion, sports, pleasure, food, clothes, education, fame)
How can these become idols?
Explain:

What can we do to keep them from becoming idols in our lives?

Read Deuteronomy 32:15-17. Jeshurun means upright one and is referring to the nation of Israel. What does it say they were sacrificing to when they worshiped idols? (verse 17)

How is idolatry the worship of demons?

Idolatry is setting your heart on something other than God. What kinds of things can we do to protect ourselves from idolatry?

In verse 5 of Exodus 20, the punishment on the children for idolatry is to the third and fourth generations. Who does it say is responsible, "for the sin of the _____."

How many generations can be blessed if we love God and keep His commands?

Based on this LIFE TRUTH which idol do you need to watch out for the most? How can you help others to obey this command?

CIVIL GOVERNMENT
LIFE TRUTH # 3
YOU SHALL NOT MISUSE
THE NAME OF THE LORD

We have learned from the first two commandments that our worship must be to God and God alone. Our hearts should never be in pursuit of anything more than God. Our allegiance must be to Him. It is for our benefit to know God and understand His character. By studying a perfect God, we are then able to become more perfect.

If we pattern our lives after the life of Christ, and live by His commands and teachings, we can become great leaders and great citizens. Why? Because God is perfect and holy. He never makes mistakes and He never makes an ungodly decision. When we focus on His culture and His character, we learn to become all that God has created us to be. It is for our own benefit to pursue God and become more like Him. What if you were told that your young son had been chosen to one day be the leader of a great nation? You knew that when he turned 17, he would be taken to lead the nation. What would you do? Most likely, you would do all that you could to teach him leadership, public speaking, reasoning, discernment, and management skills. You would want to prepare him to govern wisely, justly, and righteously. You would tell him to be aware of people who might want to take over the throne for selfish gain. So would you hire a tutor? Would you look for a mentor? Perhaps, but the best thing you could do for him would be to teach him to follow the example of Christ.

When great people die, we reflect on their lives and remember the great acts of love, sacrifice, and devotion that they displayed. We admire them and recall the things they did. We also refer to them by name. For example, Josh was a great husband and father. He sacrificed for his family and always made time for his children. He was a man of his word and was always willing to help someone in need. It would be a terrible thing if people went around saying awful statements about him, unfairly discrediting his name and his reputation.

The same is true for God. God is perfect and holy. His name should never be misused or profaned. He has never done anything wrong nor has any evil ever come from Him. There is nothing negative to say about him. His name is to be highly respected and used in reverence only. Our command to not misuse God's name goes much deeper than just connecting His name with a curse word or calling out his name in vain. It has to do with the character we display when we call him our Lord.

Using God's name carelessly or frivolously is sinful. Many people say, "Oh my _____." This is misusing God's name. They are not calling out to Him in prayer or speaking His name with reverence. It is just a frivolous phrase. If we are going to address God, then we need to address Him. We are not to just throw out His name when we are surprised, angry, or confused. If we call out to Him, we should have something to say. We should only speak His name with respect and reverence.

Would you be careless as to how you addressed a police officer? Would you use curse words and speak carelessly? If you did, you'd most likely get a warning or a more serious consequence for doing so.
God is the ultimate authority. He is to be respected at all times. He is a spirit. His presence is everywhere. We must be careful to honor and respect His name at all times.

The third command comes with a specific warning. *Exodus 20:7 (NIV)* [7] *"You shall not misuse the name of the LORD your God, for the LORD will not hold anyone guiltless who misuses his name.*

You will receive a consequence if you misuse God's name. God will not overlook this offense. You will be charged guilty.

Old Testament names have meanings. Joshua means "The Lord saves." David means "beloved." Jeremiah means "May Yahweh lift up." Isaiah means "Yahweh saves." Sometimes God changed a person's name to represent more of their character; the person who God had called them to be. God changed Abram, which means "Exalted Father," to Abraham, which means "Father of a multitude." In the New Testament, Jesus changed Simon's name to Peter, which means "rock". Peter became a rock for the establishment of the early church.

God has many names. His names reveal His character. El is a name used for God that means *mighty*. El-Shaddai means "The Almighty God." Yahweh is another name for God. It means *everlasting one* or *present one*. Yahweh-Shalom means the "Lord is peace." Yahweh-Jireh means the "Lord will provide." *Genesis 22:14 (NIV) 14 So Abraham called that place The LORD Will Provide. And to this day it is said, "On the mountain of the LORD it will be provided."* Not one of God's names reveals a flaw or anything negative about Him in any way. God is the Holy One. There is none like Him. No one deserves more respect than Him. There will never be anything negative to say about God. Some may lie about Him. Some may try to portray Him in a negative light. But all things will be revealed about Him on the Day of Judgment. God will be proven to be holy, righteous, and without sin.

Satan tries to discredit God's name with lies. He wants us to distrust His commands. Satan chose to lie to Adam and Eve in the garden so they would doubt the words of God. He alluded to the fact that God didn't want them to eat the fruit for fear that they would become like God. Satan misrepresented God and misused His name. God's commands are perfect, not deceptive. They are given for our benefit. God wants us to become more like Him. If we pattern our lives after Christ, we will be blessed. Our families will be blessed. This nation will be blessed.

We began with the illustration of how to raise a son to be a great leader. We learned that our focus must be on Christ, His character, and His teachings. If our goal was to be a great athlete, we'd look at successful athletes and imitate them. We'd strive to do what they were doing. In the same way, we need to imitate Christ so that we can learn to become more like Him.

How can we misuse God's name?

1. Use it carelessly

Using God's name carelessly is a sin. His name should never be used *as* or *with* a curse word. Saying God's name carelessly, robs God of the reverence that He deserves. God's name should only be used in reverence or in prayer. Our words need to bring glory to God. *Colossians 3:17 (NIV)* [17] *And whatever you do, whether in word or deed, do it all in the name of the Lord Jesus, giving thanks to God the Father through him.* Everything we do should bring glory to God.

2. Live hypocritical lives

Paul warns us, and the church in Rome, not to blaspheme God's name by the way we live our lives.

The Jews knew the commands of God. They knew how to live holy lives and be examples to the people around them. God gave them laws to help perfect them and teach them how to be holy. The Jewish people knew that through their actions, God's name would be respected. Neighboring nations would see righteousness, blessings, love, and unity among the Jewish people and would be amazed at the awesome God they served.

The Jews knew that if they disobeyed God's laws, they would bring contempt, disrespect, and dishonor to God. This is what it means to blaspheme God. *Romans 2:17-24 (NIV) 17 Now you, if you call yourself a Jew; if you rely on the law and brag about your relationship to God; 18 if you know his will and approve of what is superior because you are instructed by the law; 19 if you are convinced that you are a guide for the blind, a light for those who are in the dark, 20 an instructor of the foolish, a teacher of infants, because you have in the law the embodiment of knowledge and truth— 21 you, then, who teach others, do you not teach yourself? You who preach against stealing, do you steal? 22 You who say that people should not commit adultery, do you commit adultery? You who abhor idols, do you rob temples? 23 You who brag about the law, do you dishonor God by breaking the law? 24 As it is written: "God's name is blasphemed among the Gentiles because of you."*

As Christians, we say that we are Christ followers. The very word Christian means Christ-like. If we call

ourselves Christians and do things that go against God's law, we blaspheme God's name.
2 Timothy 2:19 (NIV) [19] Nevertheless, God's solid foundation stands firm, sealed with this inscription: "The Lord knows those who are his," and, "Everyone who confesses the name of the Lord must turn away from wickedness."

When we become Christians, we take on the name of Christ. We become His children and are expected to act like Him. Children who are disrespectful, rude, and unruly do not behave in a godly manner. *Ephesians 5:1 (NIV) [1] Be imitators of God, therefore, as dearly loved children...*

In speaking to slaves, Paul tells them to be respectful and honor the authorities over them. This passage is a reminder for us to be respectful to all authorities. This includes our employers. If we are not being respectful employees, then we are slandering God's name. We are not obeying God's commands. *I Timothy 6:1 (NIV) [1] All who are under the yoke of slavery should consider their masters worthy of full respect, so that God's name and our teaching may not be slandered.*

God's Word calls people who claim to be Christians, yet live contrary to His commands, liars. As we talked about in the first commandment, the law is holy, but it does not save us. The law reveals to us our sins and our need for Christ's sacrificial atonement. As we make Jesus our Lord, we become filled with the Holy Spirit. This enables us to obey the law and bring praise to God's name by how we live. *I John 2:3-6 (NIV)* ³ *We know that we have come to know him if we obey his commands.* ⁴ *The man who says, "I know him," but does not do what he commands is a liar, and the truth is not in him.* ⁵ *But if anyone obeys his word, God's love is truly made complete in him. This is how we know we are in him:* ⁶ *Whoever claims to live in him must walk as Jesus did.*

3. Forget about its power

Satan has been trying to destroy Jesus ever since He has been born. *Matthew 2:13,16 (NIV)* ¹³ *When they had gone, an angel of the Lord appeared to Joseph in a dream. "Get up," he said, "take the child and his mother and escape to Egypt. Stay there until I tell you, for Herod is going to search for the child to kill him." ...* ¹⁶ *When Herod realized that he had been outwitted by the Magi, he was furious. He gave orders to kill all the boys in Bethlehem, and its vicinity, who were two years old and younger.* This was in accordance with the timeframe he had learned from the Magi.
Herod might have been the one who gave the orders, but it was Satan who filled his heart to do such a hideous thing. The motive was to kill Jesus and stop His reign. But Satan will never overcome the reign of Jesus. He can only destroy lives by getting people to forget the one name that will save them. The Bible speaks about Jesus in *Acts 4:12 (NIV)* ¹² *Salvation is found in no one else, for there is no other name under heaven given to men by which we must be saved."*

Satan tries to get generations to silence the name of Jesus. As generations do, they suffer the consequences. Our government says that we must not pray in school, talk about the Bible, or pray in the name of Jesus at public events. If we take the name of Jesus out of our lives, we remove the only power that we have to be righteous. Our ability to live upright and godly lives, is Christ in us. Without Christ in us, we will remain trapped in our sinful flesh unable to obey God's law.

To silence the name of Jesus is detrimental to any nation. Without Christ, this country will continue down the morality ladder. Idolatry will thrive and lead to more and more detestable things like pornography, adultery, murder, rape, drugs, greed, etc. We cannot be free unless we call upon the name of Jesus!

How can we turn our nation around? Christ and Christ alone. We have forgotten that the greatest and most powerful name is Jesus. Paul speaks about Jesus in *Philippians 2:9-10 (NIV)* *⁹ Therefore God exalted him to the highest place and gave him the name that is above every name, ¹⁰ that at the name of Jesus every knee should bow, in heaven and on earth and under the earth,*

Righteousness comes through the name of Jesus alone. *2 Thessalonians 1:12 (NIV)* *¹² We pray this so that the name of our Lord Jesus may be glorified in you,* and you in him, according to the grace of our God and the Lord Jesus Christ.

When we come together as the body of Christ, we come together under the name and authority of Jesus. Look at what Paul says in *I Corinthians 5:4 (NIV)* ⁴ *When you are assembled in the name of our Lord Jesus and I am with you in spirit, and the power of our Lord Jesus is present...*

There is power in the name of Jesus. *Acts 4:7-10 (NIV)* ⁷ *They had Peter and John brought before them and began to question them: "By what power or what name did you do this?"* ⁸ *Then Peter, filled with the Holy Spirit, said to them: "Rulers and elders of the people!* ⁹ *If we are being called to account today for an act of kindness shown to a cripple and are asked how he was healed,* ¹⁰ *then know this, you and all the people of Israel: It is by the name of Jesus Christ of Nazareth, whom you crucified but whom God raised from the dead, that this man stands before you healed.*

Satan wants to silence the name of Jesus because it is the power of God unto salvation. *John 11:25-26 (NIV)* ²⁵ *Jesus said to her, "I am the resurrection and the life. He who believes in me will live, even though he dies;* ²⁶ *and whoever lives and believes in me will never die. Do you believe this?"*

John 14:6 (NIV) ⁶ *Jesus answered, "I am the way and the truth and the life. No one comes to the Father except through me.*

Those who want to silence the name of Jesus have sided with Satan. They want to destroy our only hope of salvation. Label people however you want: republican, democrat, liberal, conservative. There are only two real sides. Those who side with Jesus and those who side with Satan. If you decide to be silent about the name of Jesus, then you have decided to side with Satan. *Romans 14:11-12 (NIV) [11] It is written: "'As surely as I live,' says the Lord, 'every knee will bow before me; every tongue will confess to God.'" [12] So then, each of us will give an account of himself to God.* On the Day of Judgment, I want to be on the side of Jesus! I am NOT concerned about being politically correct in this world. I am concerned about getting into heaven and being with Jesus forever!

A passage in Acts reminds us of the faith of the Apostles and the early church. Satan was trying to silence the name of Jesus in that generation as well. The apostles were warned in, *Acts 4:17-18 (NIV) [17] But to stop this thing from spreading any further among the people, we must warn these men to speak no longer to anyone in this name." [18] Then they called them in again and commanded them not to speak or teach at all in the name of Jesus.*

The apostles did not stop, so the government beat them and threw them in prison to silence them. Many nations have experienced this type of persecution. When governments tell their people not to speak the name of Jesus, nations begin to suffer and fall. If our country continues down this same path of silencing the name of Jesus, then our sufferings will increase and our nation will fall. The apostles did not follow the politically correct path. They knew the only hope for a nation was the power in Jesus name. A miracle happened when they were freed from prison. Instead of thinking of their own safety and comfort, the apostles went right back into the streets and began teaching in Jesus name.

The passage says in *Acts 5:25-29 (NIV)* *[25] Then someone came and said, "Look! The men you put in jail are standing in the temple courts teaching the people." [26] At that, the captain went with his officers and brought the apostles. They did not use force, because they feared that the people would stone them. [27] Having brought the apostles, they made them appear before the Sanhedrin to be questioned by the high priest. [28] "We gave you strict orders not to teach in this name," he said. "Yet you have filled Jerusalem with your teaching and are determined to make us guilty of this man's blood."*

The apostles response to the government officials should be our response today! *[29] Peter and the other apostles replied: "We must obey God rather than men! There is no other name that can free us from our sins! There is no other name that can enable us to live righteous lives! There is no other name unto salvation!* **Don't be silent about Jesus! Jesus is the only hope for every nation!** *Acts 10:43 (NIV) [43] All the prophets testify about him (Jesus) that everyone who believes in him receives forgiveness of sins through his name."*

65

The name of Jesus is powerful. Satan wants to silence it. Have you seen news reports where people are told they cannot pray in Jesus name? Sometimes they're even told they can pray to God, but not to Jesus. Sometimes they're told they cannot pray at all. The greatest power we have is to pray in Jesus name. Jesus said this in John 14:12-14 (NIV) 12, *I tell you the truth, anyone who has faith in me will do what I have been doing. He will do even greater things than these, because I am going to the Father. 13 And I will do whatever you ask in my name, so that the Son may bring glory to the Father. 14 You may ask me for anything in my name, and I will do it.*

The church has forgotten the power in Jesus name. We have misused God's name by forgetting about the importance of His name. Church prayer meetings are quickly becoming a thing of the past. When was the last time you went to a church prayer meeting? When was the last time that your church held a fast? We need to remember the power we have when we gather together to pray in Jesus name. Churches have become more focused on events and activities and less on the importance of prayer. Jesus said that His house is to be a house of prayer.

Are you tired of seeing our nation crumble? Are you tired of the rise in violence, crime, and other immoralities? Then tell everyone about the name of Jesus and how they can be saved! Pray in Jesus name and see the results.

Psalm 113:2-4 (NIV) ² *Let the name of the LORD be praised, both now and forevermore.* ³ *From the rising of the sun to the place where it sets, the name of the LORD is to be praised.* ⁴ *The LORD is exalted over all the nations, his glory above the heavens.*

Proverbs 18:10 (NIV) ¹⁰ *The name of the LORD is a strong tower; the righteous run to it and are safe.*

Psalm 8:9 (NIV) ⁹ *O LORD, our Lord, how majestic is your name in all the earth!*

Romans 10:9-10 (NIV) ⁹ *That if you confess with your mouth, "Jesus is Lord," and believe in your heart that God raised him from the dead, you will be saved.* ¹⁰ *For it is with your heart that you believe and are justified, and it is with your mouth that you confess and are saved.*
Acts 3:19 (NIV) ¹⁹ *Repent, then, and turn to God, so that your sins may be wiped out, that times of refreshing may come from the Lord,*
Exodus 20:7 (NIV) ⁷ *"You shall not misuse the name of the LORD your God, for the LORD will not hold anyone guiltless who misuses his name.*

Are you ready for a change in your life? Are you tired of being in bondage to your sin? Then call upon the name of Jesus and be saved. **THERE IS POWER IN THE NAME OF JESUS!**

WORKSHEET FOR CIVIL GOVERNMENT
LIFE TRUTH # 3
YOU SHALL NOT MISUSE
THE NAME OF THE LORD

Question: What does it mean to misuse God's name?
Answer: We can misuse God's name in our speech, in our actions, and when we forget about its power.

Exodus 20:7 (NIV) 7 "You shall not misuse the name of the LORD your God, for the LORD will not hold anyone guiltless who misuses his name.

> Write out the Life Truth, question, and answer on one side of an index card and the verse on the other side. Keep it in your Bible for the week. Work on it every day individually and as a family. Have it memorized by next week.

The word misuse means having no value or importance. Why is it a sin to use God's name with no value or importance?

Read Hebrews 12:28. How does this help us understand how we are to use God's name?
In our generation, how have you seen God's name used in vain?

When your name is mentioned, what do you think are some of the first thoughts of people? (kind, giver, selfish, quiet, Christian, etc...)

What words would you like people to think about you?

What can you do to make this a reality? (Hint: Galatians 5:16; 2 Corinthians 5:15)

Read Romans 2:17-24. When we get saved, we take on the name of Christ. How does this passage say we can misuse His name?

Bearing God's holy name is a great responsibility. What kinds of things do we need to be aware of to handle this responsibility correctly?

Misusing God's name is also forgetting about the power in God's name. Read John 1:12; 3:18 What power comes from His name in these passages? Read Acts 4:8-10. What power comes from His name in this passage?

Read Acts 4:16-20. Satan is always trying to get people not to speak or teach in the name of Jesus. In what ways do you see him doing this in our generation?

Read Acts 1:14; 2:42. Does your church have a prayer service? Do you attend? Why or why not?

Based on this LIFE TRUTH which area of misusing God's name do you need to watch out for the most (speech, actions, forgetting about its power)? How can you help others to obey this command?

CIVIL GOVERNMENT
LIFE TRUTH # 4
REMEMBER THE SABBATH DAY
BY KEEPING IT HOLY

The first four of the Ten Commandments teach us how to love God. The last six of the commandments teach us how to love others. Jesus says in *Matthew 22:37-40 (NIV)* *37 Jesus replied: "'Love the Lord your God with all your heart and with all your soul and with all your mind.' 38 This is the first and greatest commandment. 39 And the second is like it: 'Love your neighbor as yourself.' 40 All the Law and the Prophets hang on these two commandments."*

The first three commandments begin with *"you shall not."* But the fourth commandment begins with *"remember".* Remember that God rested from His labor at creation, thereby establishing a rule for all of humanity to obey. He says, *"Remember the Sabbath day by keeping it holy."*

From the very beginning, God's design was for man to work six days and then rest from his labors on the seventh. Jesus reminds us of God's plan in the New Testament. *Mark 2:27 (NIV)* *27 Then he said to them, "The Sabbath was made for man, not man for the Sabbath."* God established the Sabbath for our benefit. It is medically proven that we need to rest. Productivity levels increase when we rest on the seventh day.

Several countries have tried to alter God's work plan. France tried to move away from God's plan by establishing a 10 day work week. Their new plan failed miserably. The Soviet Union tried different ways to break the fourth commandment as well. They tried seven days of work and then a day of rest. They tried eight work days and then a day of rest. To their surprise, but not to God's, these new plans didn't work. They finally returned to the Biblical pattern of six work days and then a day of rest.

Rest from work is for our benefit. We need to thank God and show Him that we love Him by obeying this command. Jesus said in *John 14:15 (NIV)* [15] *"If you love me, you will obey what I command.* We can trust God. We know that He desires to bless us and provide for us. Keeping the Sabbath holy is a command He gave to help us.

Ways to honor the Sabbath have been debated for generations. People have had a variety of views on how to keep the Sabbath holy; or even whether to keep it holy at all. The Bible tells us in the New Testament that the Ten Commandments are laws that still need to be obeyed today. Satan is always at work trying to deceive us. He wants us to disobey God's commands. He knows that if we do, things will not go well for us.

The founders of America were very committed to obeying ALL of the Ten Commandments and the teachings of Christ. In 1846, S.A. Benjamin broke the command to keep the Sabbath holy. The South Carolina Supreme Court ruled, *"The Lord's day, the day of the resurrection, is to us, who are called Christians, the day of rest after finishing a new creation. It is the first visible triumph over death, hell, and the grave!...On that day we rest, and to us it is the Sabbath of the Lord – its decent observance, in a Christian community, is that which ought to be expected."*

From 1846 until today, this country has dramatically changed. Society has continued to move further away from God's law. Our disobedience to the Sabbath command has had a great deal to do with the condition we are in. It bears repeating that we must return to this command, both individually and as a nation, in order to begin a healing. There are civil lessons, plus God's perfect design for man, in this command. It is a safeguard for us to repeat God's truth. Look at what Paul said in *Philippians 3:1 (NIV)*
[1] *Finally, my brothers, rejoice in the Lord! It is no trouble for me to write the same things to you again, and it is a safeguard for you.*

The founders of America were a Biblically-based group. The Bible was the only book they needed to help build this nation. Providence was a word they used often; meaning God's guidance and care. No church or government was ever going to rule them again. The Bible was their source of strength. They knew that if they obeyed the laws of God, He would bless them and guide them.

It is not a mystery why God blessed America. He blesses a nation that puts Him and His laws first. The founders were not blessed because they wrote the Constitution. They were blessed because they obeyed the commands of God. Our commitment to obedience is not the same today. This country is in desperate need of healing and restoration. We need to put Him and His commands first once again.

Are we missing something that the founders understood? I believe that we have forgotten to remember the Sabbath day by keeping it holy. Our generation says it is okay to work, cause others to work, purchase things, go to sporting events, and pretty much do whatever we want on the Sabbath. Many Christians routinely break the Sabbath commandment. Christian speakers and leaders travel on Sundays, sell books on Sundays, and eat out on Sundays. There isn't one founder of America who would have agreed to this kind of desecration on the Lord's Day.

I mentioned earlier about the case between S.A. Benjamin and the South Carolina Supreme Court. In 1801, Charleston passed a law stating that nothing should be sold on Sunday, the Christian Sabbath. S. A. Benjamin sold one pair of gloves on the Christian Sabbath and was found guilty and fined by the South Carolina Supreme Court. By 1846, the South Carolina Supreme Court arrested and prosecuted all offenders of the fourth commandment. The laws in this country were also written to keep businesses closed in honor of the Lord's Day until the 1980s.

Some people today think that you can choose your own Sabbath. Why were the founders so committed to the Christian Sabbath being on Sunday? In the commandment, the word "day" is singular not plural. It does not say remember the Sabbath *days* and keep *them* holy. It does not give us the option, as a people or a nation, to choose our own day. It says we work six days and then we rest on the seventh. The command is not for each of us to choose which day to rest. One of the main purposes of the day is corporate worship. This fact was clearly understood both in the Old and New Testament.

The command does not say that Saturday is the Sabbath. It says, *"Six days you shall labor and do all your work, but the seventh day is a Sabbath to the LORD your God."* This was intentional by God. He knew the day would change from Saturday to Sunday, as the apostles exampled for us, in the New Testament. But what about other religions? Will Jesus accept people that do not believe that He is God? *John 8:23-25 (NIV)* [23] *But he continued, "You are from below; I am from above. You are of this world; I am not of this world.* [24] *I told you that you would die in your sins; if you do not believe that I am [the one I claim to be], you will indeed die in your sins."* [25] *"Who are you?" they asked. "Just what I have been claiming all along," Jesus replied.*

Who did Jesus claim to be? He says in *John 14:9 (NIV) Anyone who has seen me has seen the Father.* Jesus claimed to be the one and only true God. Therefore, we must obey Him and submit to His authority. Christians recognize the Sabbath as Sunday. Therefore, we are to keep Sundays holy. We need to follow the example of our founding fathers and return to obeying this commandment the way it is written.

Should a nation seek to enforce the Sabbath law? Yes. A nation should seek to enforce moral standards by teaching its people how to be holy. Did God enforce His laws upon the nation of Israel? Were there specific consequences for breaking God's laws? Yes! We have God's laws to protect morality in this world. The Sabbath is just one of the ten moral laws that God instructed us to live by. This nation used to encourage the memorization of Scripture and the teachings of the Ten Commandments. Today, we like to memorize cliff notes and decide for ourselves what the command means. The Sabbath commandment is the longest of all the Ten Commandments. It is very specific about how we are to obey it.

Exodus 20:8-11 (NIV) [8] "Remember the Sabbath day by keeping it holy. [9] Six days you shall labor and do all your work, [10] but the seventh day is a Sabbath to the LORD your God. On it you shall not do any work, neither you, nor your son or daughter, nor your manservant or maidservant, nor your animals, nor the alien within your gates. *¹¹ For in six days the LORD made the heavens and the earth, the sea, and all that is in them, but he rested on the seventh day. Therefore the LORD blessed the Sabbath day and made it holy.*

Our generation justifies working and doing things that cause others to work on the Sabbath. We embrace activities on the Sabbath. These actions cause many to turn their devotion and love away from God. Businesses should close. Breaking this commandment by causing others to work, or working ourselves, desecrates His special day. Just think about Super Bowl Sunday. Its popularity grows every year. In 2014, 111.5 million people watched the Super Bowl. Thousands work to make it happen. Many people worship teams instead of God. It's a huge draw for gambling, prostitution, drunkenness, and other evils. Often the commercials are filled with lust and covetousness. The half-time shows are far from wholesome family entertainment. Not one of our founders would have supported an event like this on the Lord's Day. In fact, they would have sought strict legislation to stop the breaking of God's law.

It's no coincidence that things like the Super Bowl are on a Sunday. Satan is always at work tempting us to break God's commands. My old nature would love to watch the Super Bowl and to be entertained on the Lord's Day. But my new nature listens to the Spirit of God and seeks to remember the Sabbath day by keeping it holy. This means to keep the whole day holy. It does not mean to attend church for an hour and then do as you please for the rest of the day. What does holy mean to you? Are you keeping the whole day holy?

Timothy Dwight was an American educator and author. He was president of Yale when it was a Biblically-based university from 1795-1817. He delivered a speech on July 4, 1798, entitled, *The Duty of Americans, at the Present Crisis*. He said, *"To destroy us therefore, in this dreadful sense, our enemies must first destroy our Sabbath and seduce us from the house of God."* Timothy Dwight was explaining how Voltaire's atheism inspired the French Revolution's Reign of Terror where 40,000 people were beheaded. He went on to say, *"If our religion were gone, our state of society would perish with it and nothing would be left which would be worth defending."*

When we remove religion and morality from society; society will destroy itself. The founders understood this. We need to return to our Christian roots and follow the example our founders laid out for us. They spoke often about God's providence. Baker's Encyclopedia says this about providence: *God's activity throughout history in providing for the needs of human beings, especially those who follow him in faith.*

God's Word promises blessings for obedience and curses for disobedience. When we obey the Ten Commandments and the teachings of Christ, we will be blessed. If we disobey the commands, we will be cursed. This is why the founders wrote laws that helped people obey the laws of God. They wanted God's providence. A pastor during the founding era, John Prince, wrote, "*May a sense of the dangers which hang over us lead us to repentance, and fervent prayer, that God may turn from us these tokens of His anger, and cause us more highly to esteem and improve, in future, His spiritual and temporal blessings.*"

Can you see the dangers which hang over us? Are you willing to deny yourself the pleasures of this world and love God by obeying the first four commandments? Deuteronomy 28:1-3 (NIV) [1] *If you fully obey the LORD your God and carefully follow all his commands I give you today, the LORD your God will set you high above all the nations on earth.* [2] *All these blessings will come upon you and accompany you if you obey the LORD your God:* [3] *You will be blessed in the city and blessed in the country.*

In Numbers, Chapter 11, the Israelites were complaining about food and being left out in the desert. God told Moses to tell the people that He was going to give them meat to eat. Moses questioned God because they were in the desert and said, "*even if they slaughtered all the animals that wouldn't be enough to feed them all.*" I love God's answer in Numbers 11:23 (NIV) [23] *The LORD answered Moses, "Is the LORD's arm too short? You will now see whether or not what I say will come true for you."*

God sent a mighty wind that brought three feet of quail all around the Israelites. Three feet of quail! Was the Lord's arm too short? No! God can do what God wants to do. He blesses nations that carefully obey His commands. The founders got it! They fought hard to make sure that all the commandments were obeyed; just as they were written.

One of the foundational pillars to the success of our free nation is to keep the Sabbath holy. It is a day for corporate worship, instruction, and accountability; so that we will not stray from God's commands. The Sabbath is the glue that keeps the church and the nation together. Families, churches, and nations will be blessed by keeping the day holy.

By obeying this commandment, we set ourselves apart from an increasingly secular society. It is an opportunity for us to be an example to the world; a testimony to reveal that Jesus is our Lord. It is a commandment that preachers need to be preaching today.

Let's break the commandment down.

1. Keep the Sabbath holy - *"Remember the Sabbath day by keeping it holy."*

Every week we are to remember that God's day is to be kept holy. This means that we are to refrain from all secular duties that can be done the day before or the day after. The founders refrained from amusements, traveling, business, and even idle talk. They committed themselves to being devoted to the duties of public and private worship. Our generation would accuse them of being boring, but they cried out like David in *Psalm 122:1 (NIV) I rejoiced with those who said to me, "Let us go to the house of the LORD."* Which would you rather do? Attend a prayer and praise meeting on a Sunday night for corporate worship or watch the Super Bowl? Perhaps the question should be rephrased. Which should you do? What do you think the founders would have chosen? What do you think Jesus would choose?

The Lord's Day is like Jesus' birthday party. Everyone is invited. He is so awesome that He deserves a party every week! (Every day for that matter!) We come to bring Him gifts and celebrate who He is. If we miss church, it is like saying to Jesus, *"We had something better to do than come and celebrate who you are."*

Work six days - *"Six days you shall labor and do all your work"* This is the first time we learn from the commandments that God expects us to work. In the Self-Government Life Truth #10, we learned that we are created to work. God expects his creations to work and be productive in society. When we are not working and being productive in society, we are breaking a stipulation in the fourth commandment. *I Thessalonians 4:11-12 (NIV) [11] Make it your ambition to lead a quiet life, to mind your own business and to work with your hands, just as we told you, [12] so that your daily*

81

life may win the respect of outsiders and so that you will not be dependent on anybody.

We also know that all of the work is to be done in six days. We must make preparations for the Sabbath so that we do not work on God's holy day. We need to make our travel arrangements, buy our food, get our gas, or whatever else needs to be done, so that we can keep the Sabbath holy. What if it's cold and you need a pair of gloves on the Sabbath? Ask the South Carolina Supreme Court of 1864. Emergencies are the only reason a person needs to work on the Sabbath.

> **2. Lead your family – "but the seventh day is a Sabbath to the LORD your God. On it you shall not do any work, neither you, nor your son or daughter, nor your manservant or maidservant, nor your animals"**

In the second commandment, we learn that children are punished for the sins of the fathers to the third and the fourth generations. The Sabbath commandment calls for fathers to lead in the homes. The word Sabbath means to cease or desist. We are told to cease from any work on the Lord's Day. Not only are we to example a day where all secular business is not performed, but fathers are called to lead their families in this day as well. The command gives this authority to the fathers. Fathers are to set the example and lead their families to obey the

command. If the father does not keep the Sabbath holy, his family will follow right after him.
The Sabbath is a day to remember who God is. It is designed to honor and worship Him, not only publically, but also privately. The Sabbath is a day for families to attend church together. In earlier times, families worshiped, ate lunch, and spent Sabbath days together. Many would stay for an evening prayer service as well.

This generation needs fathers to lead their families by honoring the Sabbath the way God intended. The condition of the family is directly tied to the disobedience of this command. Remember, God made this command for our benefit. We need a day of rest. We need a day for worship and family fellowship.

Remembering the Sabbath Brings a Harvest of Righteousness.

The Sabbath is a time to sow a seed for righteousness. This is the same principle as planting a seed in the ground and waiting for God to produce a plant or a flower. However, there is a difference between the plant seed and the Sabbath seed. A plant seed produces a flower or a plant; the Sabbath seed produces a harvest of righteousness.
Exodus 31:12-17 (NIV) [12] *Then the LORD said to Moses,* [13] *"Say to the Israelites, 'You must observe my Sabbaths. This will be a sign between me and you for the generations to come, so you may know that* **I am the**

LORD, who makes you holy. [14] "'Observe the Sabbath, because **it is holy to you.** Anyone who desecrates it must be put to death; whoever does any work on that day must be cut off from his people. [15] For six days, work is to be done, but the seventh day is a Sabbath of rest, holy to the LORD. Whoever does any work on the Sabbath day must be put to death. [16] The Israelites are to observe the Sabbath, celebrating it for the generations to come as a **lasting covenant.** [17] **It will be a sign between me and the Israelites forever,** for in six days the LORD made the heavens and the earth, and on the seventh day he abstained from work and rested.'"

We plant the seed of righteousness when we keep the whole day holy. God promises to make us holy for our obedience. We plant it with joy; longing to be changed. The Sabbath command is similar to the first two commandments in that we must love God more than anything in this world. Are we willing to turn away from all of the secular pulls of the world for one whole day a week?

I John 2:15-17 (NIV) [15] Do not love the world or anything in the world. If anyone loves the world, the love of the Father is not in him. [16] For everything in the world–the cravings of sinful man, the lust of his eyes and the boasting of what he has and does–comes not from the Father but from the world. [17] The world and its desires pass away, but the man who does the will of God lives forever.

The ones who obey God's commandments will live forever. We know that obeying God's commands does not save us; but it is the evidence that we are saved. Romans 2:13 (NIV) *¹³ For it is not those who hear the law who are righteous in God's sight, but it is those who obey the law who will be declared righteous.*

Sow the seed of righteousness and obey the Sabbath command. Watch the harvest come forth in our nation as we return to loving God more than anything in this world. Plant the seed of joy for the Lord and His Sabbath. It is a seed that produces a harvest of righteousness and joy. As Isaiah 58 says, *"if we call the Sabbath a delight."* We will not receive a harvest if we sow the seed as though God's command is a burden. The Bible says in 1 John 5:3 (NIV) *³ This is love for God: to obey his commands. And his commands are not burdensome.*

3. Lead your community and nation – *"nor the alien within your gates."*

The word *alien* refers to someone who is not an Israelite. It is a foreigner who lives in a nation or community. We are called to lead those who are not Christians and are living in our land. We must never cause them to break the command. We are to lead them to obey the laws of God.

The term *gate* means within the community. It symbolizes a town enclosed by gates for protection. The nation of Israel was to make sure that those who entered into their community obeyed the laws of God. If you were a foreigner living in an Israelite community, and you decided to get up on the Sabbath to do work, the nation would stop you. *"Nor the alien within your gate... shall do any work."* This is why they ruled as they did in Charleston SC. S. A. Benjamin's defense was that he honored the Jewish Sabbath and not the Christian Sabbath. Since Benjamin chose to reside in a Christian nation, he needed to honor the Christian Sabbath. How would you rule today? Would you stand upon the commands of God? Would you believe the lie that tells us we no longer have to obey? Would you accept the lie that says we need to tolerate all beliefs? We need to say, *"You are welcome to live in our land, but you need to obey our laws.* **Our future blessings are dependent upon our obedience to God's commands."**

4. **Follow the Lord's example -** *Exodus 20:11* **(NIV)** *¹¹ **For in six days the LORD made the heavens and the earth, the sea, and all that is in them, but he rested on the seventh day. Therefore the LORD blessed the Sabbath day and made it holy.***

God has no need of rest. It does not benefit Him at all to take a break. He has absolutely no weaknesses. He rested only for our benefit. He was setting an example for us. God never asks us to do anything that He would not do himself. He is a good God, a loving God, and a kind God. Satan lies. He tries to tell us that the Sabbath is boring or that the Sabbath commandment no longer applies to us today. He wants us to believe that we are free to do whatever we want on the Sabbath.

God's command says different, *"Remember the Sabbath day by keeping it holy."* Keep the day free from all of the secular amusements you can attend during the week. Keep the day free from all of the business you may conduct during the week. Keep the day holy by attending public worship services. Keep the day holy by spending it with your family. Keep the day holy by resting so you can be ready to work productively for the next six days.

5. **God created you to be free – *"neither you, nor your son or daughter, nor your manservant or maidservant, nor your animals."***

In this command, we learn that God desired for man to be free. He created us to be free. We are free to own our own property. This is what He desires for us: your animal, your employee, your stuff. It is brought out again in the last command. *Exodus 20:17 (NIV)* [17] *"You shall not covet your neighbor's house. You shall not covet your neighbor's wife, or his manservant or maidservant, his ox or donkey, or anything that belongs to your neighbor."* God created us to be stewards and to be responsible for our own property.

In the Declaration of Independence it says that all men are created with unalienable rights. The right to life, liberty, and the pursuit of happiness. The founders used the phrase "pursuit of happiness" to include our ability to own property. This is a God-given right.

Issues that arise with our property have to do with our obedience to God. If we obey God, we remain free to own our own property and keep certain freedoms. But if we disobey God, we lose our freedoms and our property. The judgment for disobeying God's commands is a loss of our property and a return to slavery. We can see this pattern all throughout the Old Testament.

Look at this passage in *Judges 2:8-19 (NIV)* *⁸ Joshua son of Nun, the servant of the LORD, died at the age of a hundred and ten. ⁹ And they buried him in the land of* **his inheritance**, *at Timnath Heres in the hill country of Ephraim, north of Mount Gaash. ¹⁰ After that whole generation had been gathered to their fathers, another generation grew up, who knew neither the LORD nor what he had done for Israel. ¹¹ Then the Israelites did evil in the eyes of the LORD and served the Baals. ¹² They forsook the LORD, the God of their fathers, who had brought them out of Egypt. They followed and worshiped various gods of the peoples around them. They provoked the LORD to anger ¹³ because they forsook him and served Baal and the Ashtoreths. ¹⁴* **In his anger against Israel the LORD handed them over to raiders who plundered them. He sold them to their**

enemies all around, whom they were no longer able to resist. ¹⁵ Whenever Israel went out to fight, the hand of the LORD was against them to defeat them, just as he had sworn to them. They were in great distress. ¹⁶ Then the LORD raised up judges, who saved them out of the hands of these raiders. ¹⁷ Yet they would not listen to their judges but prostituted themselves to other gods and worshiped them. Unlike their fathers, they quickly turned from the way in which their fathers had walked, **the way of obedience to the LORD's commands.** ¹⁸ Whenever the LORD raised up a judge for them, he was with the judge and saved them out of the hands of their enemies as long as the judge lived; for the LORD had compassion on them as they groaned under those who oppressed and afflicted them. ¹⁹ But when the judge died, the people returned to ways even more corrupt than those of their fathers, following other gods and serving and worshiping them. **They refused to give up their evil practices and stubborn ways.**

What will be written about America? Will people write that it started out well but then a generation grew up who knew neither the Lord or what He had done for America? That they quickly turned from the way in which their founders had walked, the way of obedience to the Lord's commands. You can be sure of this, unless we repent and turn back to the commands of God, we will continue to go into slavery and eventually be overcome by another. We will continue to lose our property and our freedoms. Can you see the enslavement growing in our nation?

God created us to be free and to own our own property. But when we turn away from His commands, we lose our freedoms and become enslaved by another. Are we gaining freedom in our nation or being oppressed by another? I am convinced that the founders had it right. We need to return to their example.

We have a choice about the Sabbath in this generation. Will you repent and begin to remember the Sabbath by keeping it holy? Or will you continue to go along with the ways of the world and desecrate God's day?

My church and family know where I stand. We agree with Joshua in *Joshua 24:14-15 (NIV)* [14] *"Now fear the LORD and serve him with all faithfulness. Throw away the gods your forefathers worshiped beyond the River and in Egypt, and serve the LORD.* [15] *But if serving the LORD seems undesirable to you, then choose for yourselves this day whom you will serve, whether the gods your forefathers served beyond the River, or the gods of the Amorites, in whose land you are living. But as for me and my household, we will serve the LORD."*

WORKSHEET FOR CIVIL GOVERNMENT
LIFE TRUTH # 4
REMEMBER THE SABBATH DAY
BY KEEPING IT HOLY

Question: What does it mean to keep the Sabbath holy?

Answer: We are to keep the day holy by not doing any work or causing others to work.

Exodus 20:8-11 (NIV) 8 "Remember the Sabbath day by keeping it holy. 9 Six days you shall labor and do all your work, 10 but the seventh day is a Sabbath to the LORD your God. On it you shall not do any work, neither you, nor your son or daughter, nor your manservant or maidservant, nor your animals, nor the alien within your gates. 11 For in six days the LORD made the heavens and the earth, the sea, and all that is in them, but he rested on the seventh day. Therefore the LORD blessed the Sabbath day and made it holy.

> Write out the Life Truth, question, and answer on one side of an index card and the verse on the other side. Keep it in your Bible for the week. Work on it every day individually and as a family. Have it memorized by next week.

Why do you think the Lord rested on the seventh day?

Read Mark 2:27. What do you think it means when Jesus says the Sabbath was made for man?

What does it show God when we keep the whole day holy?

Read Acts 20:7 What are the differences between the Jewish Sabbath and the Christian Sabbath?

The French atheist Voltaire said, "To overthrow Christianity we must overthrow the Christian Sabbath." Do you agree or disagree? Why?

How has Sunday observance changed, if at all, in your lifetime?

Have the changes brought about positive or negative changes? (blessings or curses)

Read Exodus 31:12-18 We must observe God's Sabbath. What does He promise to do if we will keep it holy?

Are we seeing our nation become more holy?

Could it be tied to our keeping the Sabbath holy? Why? Why not?

The Super Bowl is played on the Christian Sabbath every year. Is there anything about this event that would be breaking the Sabbath command?

If there is something that breaks the command should Christians participate in it? Why? Why not?

What does Jesus think about how our generation treats the fourth commandment?

Based on this LIFE TRUTH how can you do a better job of remembering the Sabbath day by keeping it holy? How can you help others to obey this command?

CIVIL GOVERNMENT
LIFE TRUTH # 5
HONOR YOUR FATHER
AND MOTHER

We learned in the fourth commandment that God desires for us to own our own property. God said, "Your animals" and in the command not to covet He said, "your neighbor's house...or anything that belongs to your neighbor."

As Christians, we understand the principle of stewardship. God owns everything. We are the stewards of His property. David said in *Psalm 24:1 (NIV)* [1] *The earth is the LORD's, and* **everything in it**, *the world, and all who live in it;*

So what does it mean when He says, "Your property?" It means that God does not want a king or a government ruling us harshly or taking things that we own. Jesus is the only King we need. He rules over us justly and graciously.

In 1 Samuel, Chapter 8, the nation of Israel wanted to be like the other nations around them. They wanted to have a king. God warned Samuel that an earthly king would confiscate their children, property, and goods for his own benefit. Samuel told the Israelites what God said, but they refused to listen. *1 Samuel 8:19-22 (NIV)* [19] *But the people refused to listen to Samuel. "No!" they said. "We want a king over us.*

²⁰ Then we will be like all the other nations, with a king to lead us and to go out before us and fight our battles." ²¹ When Samuel heard all that the people said, he repeated it before the LORD. ²² The LORD answered, "Listen to them and give them a king."

There are godly kings and godly governments; but when authorities abuse their power they become ungodly. It was never God's intention for kings and governments to become tyrannical. Tyrants are rulers who are not restrained by law or constitution. They exercise their power oppressively, harshly, and brutally.

Our American Declaration of Independence was written by thirteen colonies who joined together to form a union as a free nation. They were breaking away from the tyrannical rule of the King of Britain. It states, *"The history of the present king of Great Britain is a history of repeated injuries and usurpations, all having in direct object the establishment of an absolute Tyranny over these States. To prove this, let the facts be submitted to a candid world."* They listed over 20 harsh treatments being inflicted upon them by the king. America was formed as one nation under God; a Christian nation that wanted to be free from tyrannical rule. The most famous line in the Declaration of Independence is this, **"We hold these truths to be self-evident, that all men are created equal, that they are endowed by their Creator with certain unalienable rights, that among them are Life, Liberty, and the pursuit of Happiness."**

These God-fearing men understood God's intention for man. They sought to obey Him because they knew that God would provide for them and protect them. They established a land where people were free to own their own property; having no fear of oppression by a king or government. They prayerfully created a government that would not become a tyranny.

These godly men understood that the only way for this nation to be free was to make Jesus their king. They also understood that obedience to God's commands was the only way to stay free. We see this in the fifth commandment.

Exodus 20:12 (NIV) [12] "Honor your father and your mother, so that you may live long in the land the LORD your God is giving you. The passage is reinstated in the New Testament in *Ephesians 6:1-4 (NIV) [1] Children, obey your parents in the Lord, for this is right. [2] "Honor your father and mother"–which is the first commandment with a promise– [3] "that it may go well with you and that you may enjoy long life on the earth."*
God is not talking about the number of years here upon the earth. The command is about a principle that must be applied to keep a nation from going into bondage. The Ten Commandments were the instructions for all people and all nations to remain free. The intent of the passage, *"a long life on the earth"* or *"so that it may go well with you"* is speaking of being free from tyrannical rule.

One type of tyrannical rule is communism. Communism is when the state or government becomes the god of a nation. The state decides what is to be done or not done. It eliminates private property and takes from some of the people to distribute to others as the state sees fit. Karl Marx is the father of communism. He stated, *"My object in life is to dethrone God and destroy capitalism. People exist for the benefit of the state."*

Communism is achieved by socialism. Socialism is *big* government that controls everything. It takes money and property that belong to some and gives it to others. Our government is becoming more and more socialistic. Communism is not the answer a nation should be seeking. 135 million people and counting have been killed through communism. Hitler, Stalin, and others have come into power through socialism. When a government gains more and more power it becomes much easier for a tyrannical ruler to step in. Our nation is headed for communism. We call it "progressionism" but it's really just history repeating itself. The same thing that is happening to us has happened to other nations that have turned communistic. This communist movement has existed in our nation since the early 1900s. Today, over 20% of our politicians are a part of it. Their slogan is: *Radical Ideas, Real Politics.* Communist Party USA boasts of a very large membership. Unfortunately, these people are just repeating the mistakes of generations before them.

A book, entitled *The Naked Communist*, lists specific goals on how to bring a nation into communism. It was written in 1958 by an FBI agent. The agent identifies what must be achieved for a free nation to become a communist nation.

Here are a few of the goals:
- # 17 Get control of the schools. Use them as transmission belts for socialism. Get control of the teacher associations.
- # 20,21 Infiltrate the press. Gain control of key positions in radio, TV, and motion pictures.
- # 24 Eliminate all laws governing obscenity by calling them "censorship" and a violation of free speech and free press.
- # 25 Break down cultural standards of morality by promoting pornography in books, magazines, motion pictures, and TV.
- # 26 Present homosexuality and promiscuity as "normal, natural, and healthy."
- #27 Infiltrate the churches and replace revealed religion with "social" religion. Discredit the Bible.
- # 28 Eliminate prayer in schools because it violates the principle of "separation of church and state."
- # 40 Discredit the family as an institution. Encourage promiscuity and easy divorce.

These goals are nothing new. Look at goal #40; Discredit the family as an institution. God created the four Biblical institutions: Self, Family, Church and Civil Government. **The family institution was designed by God. It helps keep a nation free. Families are responsible to bring their children up in the training and instruction of the Lord.**

John Dewey was very influential in the development of the education system in America. Many people do not know that he spent time in Russia and studied Karl Marx. He was a socialist and an atheist. He believed that education should socialize the child to make him subject to the state. In the 1960's, the communists of our nation embraced Dewey and expounded upon his plan. They decided to get rid of God and morality in our public schools. Our current educational system now suffers from their decisions. Our schools have changed to a social justice curriculum. They are now teaching our children the way things should be done. They have removed the authority of God and His Word. They have begun to teach what seems right to them in their own eyes.

Proverbs 14:12 (NIV) *12 There is a way that seems right to a man, but in the end it leads to death.*

By moving closer and closer to communism, we are losing our God-given freedoms. Saul Alinsky wrote a book entitled, *Rules for Radicals,* which was first published in 1971. One of his goals was to get people on welfare and to be dependent upon the government. A.C.O.R.N. and other similar organizations have come from the teachings in his book.

When people go on welfare or disability they are basically saying, *"I agree with socialism. I agree with communism. I believe the state should take care of me."* Christians who care about their freedoms need to flee from dependency on the state. If you are unable to work, your family is to care for you. If your family cannot, then the church is to support you; not the state. The welfare concept is outside of God's plan for a nation. It places control in the hands of government which only leads to tyranny.

In the front of Saul Alinsky's book there is a list of credits. One in particular caught my attention. He says, *"Lest we forget at least an over-the-shoulder acknowledgement to the very first radical..."The first radical known to man who rebelled against the establishment and did it so effectively that he at least won his own kingdom – Lucifer."* He gives accolades to Satan and admits he is following in his footsteps. Satan has always been out to destroy nations. **He wants us to turn away from God. When we do, it does not go well for us. We will not live long in the land God has provided for us. The only way to keep ourselves free, as God intended, is to obey His commandments.** It is when we turn away from God and His commandments that we lose our freedoms and become enslaved by another.

The current IRS tax laws have more pages than the Bible. Big government has oppressive taxes so they can use our money as they see fit. If you stopped paying your property taxes or your personal property taxes, would you continue to own your property? Who really owns the property that God intends for you to have in our nation?
God's four Biblical institutions are building blocks for a godly and free society. We must learn our responsibilities in self-government and begin to apply the principles in our society. We must learn the family government principles and seek to honor God and obey His plan. Through God's plan and His power, we will live long in the land as the fifth commandment states.

The government may *seem* to be doing good things, but there's a fine line between protecting the righteous and overstepping a God-given authority. For example, if a meat processing plant used unsanitary practices that made people sick, the government's job would be to protect the righteous. They would punish the evil doer, not establish an oppressive health department. Recently, our health department shut down a little girl's cupcake business. They ruled that her kitchen was not certified by the health department. This is overstepping their God-given authority. Only if the little girl made people sick should the government step in to protect the righteous.

Do you see where all of this oppression is headed? Do you see all of the control that has been given to the government? It is becoming easier for a tyrant to step in and rule. One who could be as evil as Hitler, Stalin, or Voltaire.

Our freedoms are being lost because we have forgotten to put God first by obeying His laws. We must have greater self-government which comes through religion and morality.

Socialist movements come to power with lies that they are going to make our lives better. Have you heard this from our government? How do we have long lives in the land that Lord gives us? We honor our father and mother. We raise our children in the training and instruction of the Lord.

Where does morality come from? Satan wants people to believe that morality comes from within their own hearts. Many Christians might say that morality comes from the Bible. The truth is that morality ultimately comes from God. He gives man a new nature. We learned in the first two commandments that the only source for maintaining morality is Christ. The Bible says in *Jeremiah 17:9 (NIV)* [9] *The heart is deceitful above all things and beyond cure. Who can understand it?* Jesus says in *Matthew 15:19 (NIV)* [19] *For out of the heart come evil thoughts, murder, adultery, sexual immorality, theft, false testimony, slander.*

The Ten Commandments reveal to us that we are sinners in need of God's forgiveness. The Commandments help lead us to Christ. When we seek His forgiveness, we receive new hearts that enable us to live moral lives. We will be blessed by God if we obey His commands and walk in the training and instruction of the Lord.

Ephesians 6:1-4 (NIV) [1] Children, obey your parents in the Lord, for this is right. [2] "Honor your father and mother"--which is the first commandment with a promise-- [3] "that it may go well with you and that you may enjoy long life on the earth." [4] Fathers, do not exasperate your children; instead, bring them up in the training and instruction of the Lord.

It is all tied together. If we obey God's laws in the Biblical institutions, it will go well for us. When the nation of Israel came out of bondage in Egypt, God led them to the land of Canaan, a land flowing with milk and honey. He promised them that if they would obey Him they would live in freedom in their land.

Deuteronomy 4:9-10 (NIV) [9] Only be careful, and watch yourselves closely so that you do not forget the things your eyes have seen or let them slip from your heart as long as you live. Teach them to your children and to their children after them. [10] Remember the day you stood before the LORD your God at Horeb, when he said to me, "Assemble the people before me to hear my words so that they may learn to revere me as long as they live in the land and may teach them to their children."

Let's break the commandment down. *Exodus 20:12 (NIV) *[12]* "Honor your father and your mother, so that you may live long in the land the LORD your God is giving you.*

1. The parents responsibility in the command

The first word in the command is honor. If children are expected to honor their father and mother, then parents need to be doing all they can to be honorable. **We do not come to the fifth command by skipping the first four commandments.** Parents need to make sure that within their own lives they love God first and their allegiance and devotion is to God alone.

Parents need to be following the commands of God; not blaspheming God's name in their speech and actions. God's commandments are in perfect order. Parents need to obey the first four commands and teach and train their children to do the same. They are to instruct their children daily in the Word of God. Children should be taught by their parents to have no other gods, not to commit idolatry, not to misuse God's name, and to keep the Sabbath holy. Parents are to teach and train their children in the ways of God.

Parents today do not obey this command. The consequences of their disobedience will fall upon their children and grandchildren. The punishment will be felt to the third and the fourth generations. Parents must begin to fulfill their responsibility as the main moral instructors of their children. Homeschooling is the best option in our world today since our current public educational system is turning children against God and His standards. What do your children believe? Have they already been influenced that Biblical morality is wrong? Make the sacrifices necessary to obey God's commands and bring your children up in the Lord.

In Missouri, marriage is between one man and one woman as the Bible declares. An openly gay professor in Missouri has filed a lawsuit against the state. The law suit is seeking to change what Missouri has voted and defined a marriage to be. The ACLU claims to be the guardian of our liberty. Their goal is to extend rights to the segments of our population that have traditionally been denied their rights, including people of color; women; lesbians, gay men, bisexuals and transgender people; prisoners; and people with disabilities.

The true guardian of our liberty is God and God alone. We become and remain free when we obey Him. If we change God's definition of marriage, we are fighting against Him and His laws. Parents who neglect to teach and train their children in the ways of God will see their children side with modern philosophies. Which side of the debate would your children be on? Would they be for or against gay marriage?

The United States Congress once endorsed a Bible to be distributed throughout our nation. It was called the Aitkens Bible. Our Congress, at that time, understood that if we were to remain a free nation, parents would have to do their part by bringing their children up in the training and instruction of the Lord.

Deuteronomy 4:9 (NIV) [9] Only be careful, and watch yourselves closely so that you do not forget the things your eyes have seen or let them slip from your heart as long as you live. Teach them to your children and to their children after them.

Remember the illustration of the health department? How do you raise a young man to run his meat processing plant with integrity so he will not harm others because of greed or carelessness? It is through God's principles. His parents are responsible to teach Him to fear God and love others as he loves himself. His training would then keep him from intentionally cutting corners for wealth or laziness. He would be doing everything as unto the Lord. *Leviticus 25:17-19 (NIV) [17] Do not take advantage of each other, but fear your God. I am the LORD your God. [18] "'Follow my decrees and be careful to obey my laws, and you will live safely in the land. [19] Then the land will yield its fruit, and you will eat your fill and live there in safety.*

We have allowed God's law to slip away from our society. This generation has grown up without knowing the commands of God and their importance to our lives. Parents have neglected to teach them to their children. Today's children can't defend the principles; they can't example the principles; they can't pass on the principles. Do your children know the Ten Commandments and the teachings of Christ? Can they defend God's Word and stand against the enemy? Which side of progressive debates would they be on? God's word or worldly philosophies?

Look at what this passage says about living long in the land. *Leviticus 26:1-21 (NIV)* *[1] "'Do not make idols or set up an image or a sacred stone for yourselves, and do not place a carved stone in your land to bow down before it. I am the LORD your God. [2] "'Observe my Sabbaths and have reverence for my sanctuary. I am the LORD. [3] "'If you follow my decrees and are careful to obey my commands, [4] I will send you rain in its season, and the ground will yield its crops and the trees of the field their fruit. [5] Your threshing will continue until grape harvest and the grape harvest will continue until planting, and you will eat all the food you want and live in safety in your land. [6] "'I will grant peace in the land, and you will lie down and no one will make you afraid. I will remove savage beasts from the land, and the sword will not pass through your country. [7] You will pursue your enemies, and they will fall by the sword before you. [8] Five of you will chase a hundred, and a hundred of you will chase ten thousand, and your enemies will fall by the sword before you. [9] "'I will look on you with favor and make you fruitful and increase your numbers, and I will keep my covenant with you. [10] You will still be eating last year's harvest* when you will have to move it out to make room for the new. [11] I will put my dwelling place among you, and I will not abhor you. [12] I will walk among you and be your God, and you will be my people. [13] I am the LORD your God, who brought you out of Egypt so that you would no longer be slaves to the Egyptians; I broke the bars of your yoke and enabled you to walk with heads held high. [14] "'But if you will not listen to me and carry out all these commands, [15] and if you reject my decrees and abhor my laws and fail to carry out all my commands and so violate my covenant, [16] then I will do this to you: I will bring upon you sudden terror, wasting diseases and fever that will destroy your sight and drain away your life. You will plant seed in vain, because your enemies will eat it. [17] I will set my face against you so that you will be defeated by your enemies; those who hate you will rule over you, and you will flee even when no one is pursuing you. [18] "'If after all this you will not listen to me, I will punish you for your sins seven times over. [19] I will break down your stubborn pride and make the sky above you like iron and the ground beneath you like bronze. [20] Your strength will be spent in vain, because your soil will not yield its crops, nor will the trees of the land yield their fruit. [21] "'If you remain hostile toward me and refuse to listen to me, I will multiply your afflictions seven times over, as your sins deserve.*

2. The children's responsibility in the command

I am amazed at the number of parents who feel that if their children do not want to have a devotional time together then they should not force them. What an

==awful lie Satan has convinced parents to believe.== Some parents even believe that it turns their children away more to force them. What child if given the choice between a family devotion or a video game is going to choose the devotion? What parent if given the choice of their favorite TV show or a family devotion is going to choose the devotion?

We don't choose the training time because we always want to. We choose the devotion because it is what is best for us. This is the way to freedom. There are times when I am tired. There are times when I have had a bad day. There are times when I am busy. There are times when I would rather do something else. But my God has commanded me to teach my children His commands and His morals. If my children are choosing to side with those who think that gay marriage should be legalized, then I have done a poor job as a parent. I have neglected my responsibilities.

In an autobiography about Benjamin Franklin, it says, *"It seemed as if all the world were growing religious, so one could not walk thro' the town in an evening without hearing psalms sung in different families of every street. "* Who was leading the psalms and devotions in these homes? The parents were. They decided that they were not going to love anything more than God. They understood that they needed to bring their children up in the training and instruction of the Lord. They were living out the fifth commandment. Children when your parents are calling you to have a devotional time with them, honor them by being respectful; learning the principles that God has for you. If you do, it will go well for you and you will live long in the land. If you don't, our nation will become a tyranny. You will be enslaved by another. It is vital for our prosperity and providence that we obey the laws of our Creator. We have been endowed by God with certain unalienable rights. We must learn these rights and apply them to our lives.

If children do not respect their parents, it is very likely that they will not respect any other authority in their lives. We will excel as a loving free nation when we submit to one another out of reverence for Christ. This is the principle of loving our neighbor. It begins in the home with the children honoring their parents. Our children must heed the warnings of choosing to turn away from God. *Romans 13:10 (NIV) ¹⁰ Love does no harm to its neighbor. Therefore love is the fulfillment of the law.*

Heed the warnings children, *Deuteronomy 4:25-27 (NIV) ²⁵ After you have had children and grandchildren and have lived in the land a long time–if you then become corrupt and make any kind of idol, doing evil in the eyes of the LORD your God and provoking him to anger, ²⁶ I call heaven and earth as witnesses against you this day that you will quickly perish from the land that you are crossing the Jordan to possess. You will not live there long but will certainly be destroyed. ²⁷ The LORD will scatter you among the peoples, and only a few of you will survive among the nations to which the LORD will drive you.*

When children do not respect authority, it is a sign that they do not love God. It is a warning flag that they may not even be in the faith. When children obey and honor their parents, it is evidence that Christ is in them. They are able to learn and grow in Self-Government.

In the spring of 1630, eleven ships set sail for a new land. They traveled together for over 3000 miles. There were seven hundred men, women, and children. They risked their lives to establish a godly Puritan community. They landed in Massachusetts. John Winthrope wrote a sermon that he most likely read and studied on the journey. It was called "*A Model of Charity.*" In the sermon, he challenged the people to become the *"city on a hill"* as referred to in the New Testament. Here are his closing remarks, *"Beloved there is now set before us life, and good, death and evil in that we are commanded this day to love the Lord our God, and to love one another to walk in His ways and to keep His commandments and His ordinance, and His laws, and the articles of our covenant with Him that we may live and be multiplied, and that the Lord our God may bless us in the land whither we go to possess it. But if our hearts shall turn away so that we will not obey, but shall be seduced and worship other gods, our pleasures, and profits, and serve them; it is propounded unto us this day, we shall surely perish out of the good land whither we pass over this vast sea to possess it. Therefore, let us choose life that we, and our seed may live, by obeying His voice, and cleaving to Him, for He is our life, and our prosperity."*

The founders came with the intention of establishing a Christian nation. They understood that if they turned away from God they would no longer have God's provision and protection. If America is to remain free, we must return to God and His ways.

We are in a war against the Biblical family. We must win the war by doing what God has called us to do. We must faithfully raise the righteous.

Psalm 127:1-5 (NIV) [1] *Unless the LORD builds the house, its builders labor in vain. Unless the LORD watches over the city, the watchmen stand guard in vain.* [2] *In vain you rise early and stay up late, toiling for food to eat– for he grants sleep to those he loves.* [3] *Sons are a heritage from the LORD, children a reward from him.* [4] *Like arrows in the hands of a warrior are sons born in one's youth.* [5] *Blessed is the man whose quiver is full of them. They will not be put to shame when they contend with their enemies in the gate.*

We have neglected the Biblical education of our children. Many are not able to defend the morals of this Christian nation at the gate. Instead, our gates have allowed the enemy into our land. The enemy's agenda is to destroy this nation and its people. This has always been Satan's goal. The only way to overpower him is to repent and begin teaching and obeying the commands of God. When we do we will live long in the land the Lord has given us.

WORKSHEET FOR CIVIL GOVERNMENT
LIFE TRUTH # 5
HONOR YOUR FATHER AND MOTHER

Question: What does it mean to honor your father and mother?
Answer: Children are to learn how to respect God and others so that we can live long in the land.

Exodus 20:12 (NIV) ¹² "Honor your father and your mother, so that you may live long in the land the LORD your God is giving you.

> Write out the Life Truth, question, and answer on one side of an index card and the verse on the other side. Keep it in your Bible for the week. Work on it every day individually and as a family. Have it memorized by next week.

T or F -   The term separation of church and state is in the United States constitution.
Read Prov. 16:3; Col. 3:17. Is there ever a point when we should separate from our Christian morals?

Explain how separation of church and state is ungodly?

Read Leviticus 26:1-21. The command to honor your father and mother comes with a blessing and a promise from God. What do you think God means when He says, "so that you may live long in the land?"

How are children not honoring their parents today? In what ways do you see our culture crumbling and how can this be related to children not honoring their parents?

Deuteronomy, Chapter 5, is a restating of the Ten Commandments. Read Deuteronomy 6. What are some of the warnings in this chapter?

What do we need to do in order to remain in the land the Lord has given us?

Do you think this generation of parents is doing a good job of fulfilling their responsibility to teaching their children God's law?

How is this related to our nation's downfall?

Explain why or why not this statement is true: If children do not learn to honor their parents at home they will have issues with honoring others in authority.

Which form of government do we need more of to remain free and why? (Self / Family / Church / Civil)

Read Prov. 6:20; 13:1. How can these verses encourage children to obey their parents?

In your own words, explain what God means in the fifth commandment and how the promise is related to honoring our parents.

Based on this LIFE TRUTH, and as a parent, how will you fulfill God's requirement of teaching your children God's commands? How can you help others to obey this command?

CIVIL GOVERNMENT
LIFE TRUTH # 6
YOU SHALL NOT MURDER

Our nation needs self-government more than civil government to remain free. George Washington said, "*The foundation of our national policy will be laid in the pure and immutable principles of private morality.*" The word *immutable* means not capable of or susceptible to change. George Washington believed in the absolute truth of the Bible. He knew that private morality, or self-government, was the key to a solid national foundation. This country was birthed from these principles of morality.

Laws should discourage criminal actions and point people toward morality. Laws should punish those who commit acts that are morally wrong. The founding fathers understood this. They knew that morality and government should go hand in hand for a society to remain free. They understood that morals were completely tied to religion and to their devotion and fear of God.

I Timothy 5:4 (NIV) *⁴ But if a widow has children or grandchildren, these should learn first of all to put* **their religion into practice** *by caring for their own family and so repaying their parents and grandparents, for this is pleasing to God.*

The Northwest Ordinance was the first federal law established by Congress. It says, *"Religion, morality, and knowledge, being necessary to good government and the happiness of mankind, schools and the means of education shall forever be encouraged."* In addition, the first federal law governing the western territories said, *"Religion and morality are necessary for good government."* Our founders understood the path to a free society and carefully laid the groundwork. In September, 1789, the House of Representatives authorized the first official Thanksgiving. The resolution stated, *"A day of public thanksgiving and prayer to be observed by acknowledging with grateful hearts the many signal favors of Almighty God."* This same Congress established the First Amendment which says, *"Congress shall make no law respecting an establishment of religion, or prohibiting the free exercise thereof."* Did you know that both of these acts were done on the same day?

Some try to twist the first amendment to mean that there should be no religion at all in the civil government. This is not what the founders believed or what they established. They believed that no established religion should ever enforce laws as in Great Britain, but religious freedom should never be prohibited. They knew religion and morality were the keys to a free society.

For a nation to remain free and govern themselves fairly, there must be a set standard to live by. This set standard for a nation and a people to follow is given to us in *The Ten Commandments*.

George Washington said in his farewell address, **"Of all the dispositions and habits which lead to political prosperity, Religion and Morality are indispensable supports.** *In vain would that man claim the tribute of Patriotism, who should labor to subvert these great pillars of human happiness, these firmest props of the duties of Men and Citizens. The mere Politician, equally with the pious man, ought to respect and to cherish them. A volume could not trace all their connections with private and public felicity."* Anyone who would seek to subvert religion and morality from our government would be destroying our nation's foundation according to our first president. Washington goes on to say, *"And let us with caution indulge the supposition that morality can be maintained without religion. Whatever may be conceded to the influence of refined education on minds of peculiar structure,* **reason and experience both forbid us to expect that national morality can prevail in exclusion of religious principle."**

Our founders searched the Bible to write our laws. They sought to keep religion and morality at the forefront of their decisions. They established days of thanksgiving, days of prayer, and days of fasting to God. They endorsed the Aitken Bible and encouraged people and families to self-govern themselves in order to limit civil government and keep the people free.

They embraced the Ten Commandments and wrote laws to govern the nation according to their content. They engraved them on the capital building for all to see. They knew that in order to live long in the land the Lord God had given them, they must instruct their children in the ways of God, learn these moral commands, and apply them to their lives.

This brings us to the sixth commandment, *you shall not murder.* Murder is the intentional taking of human life. It is viewed as a serious moral crime in the Bible. Life is stated in our Declaration of Independence as something that is endowed by God. We are created in the image of God. We are created to obey, serve, glorify, and worship God. When a person intentionally takes the life of another, they commit murder and destroy a life that God intended for His glory.

Let's say you design a special vase. You spend months kneading the clay and forming it into a perfect shape. The vase is something you cherish, love, and will use for your benefit. Your love for the vase is seen in your eyes and in the care that you give it. How would it feel if you presented your vase to others and someone took it and broke it right in front of you? This is a small fraction of how God must feel when someone murders one of His precious creations.

Intentional is the key word in the definition of murder. The Bible spells it out for us. *Numbers 35:16-21 (NIV)*

¹⁶ "'If a man strikes someone with an iron object so that he dies, he is a murderer; the murderer shall be put to death. ¹⁷ Or if anyone has a stone in his hand that could kill, and he strikes someone so that he dies, he is a murderer; the murderer shall be put to death. ¹⁸ Or if anyone has a wooden object in his hand that could kill, and he hits someone so that he dies, he is a murderer; the murderer shall be put to death. ¹⁹ The avenger of blood shall put the murderer to death; when he meets him, he shall put him to death. ²⁰ If anyone with malice aforethought shoves another or throws something at him intentionally so that he dies ²¹ or if in hostility he hits him with his fist so that he dies, that person shall be put to death; he is a murderer. The avenger of blood shall put the murderer to death when he meets him.

Our laws against murder correspond with what the Scriptures teach. For death penalty cases, our courts decide if the killing was intentional or unintentional. Numbers 35:22-29 (NIV) ²² "'But if without hostility someone suddenly shoves another or throws something at him unintentionally ²³ or, without seeing him, drops a stone on him that could kill him, and he dies, then since he was not his enemy and he did not intend to harm him, ²⁴ the assembly must judge between him and the avenger of blood according to these regulations. ²⁵ The assembly must protect the one accused of murder from the avenger of blood and send him back to the city of refuge to which he fled. He must stay there until the death of the high priest, who was anointed with the holy oil. ²⁶ "'But if the accused ever goes outside the limits of the city of refuge to which he has fled ²⁷ and the avenger of blood finds *him outside the city, the avenger of blood may kill the accused without being guilty of murder. ²⁸ The accused must stay in his city of refuge until the death of the high priest; only after the death of the high priest may he return to his own property. ²⁹ "'These are to be legal requirements for you throughout the generations to come, wherever you live.*

The "assembly" protects the one accused of murder from the avenger of blood. The assembly is our court system. The city of refuge is our prison system. The person who commits murder unintentionally must still face consequences and is to be taken to the city of refuge. In Biblical times, they stayed there until the death of the high priest. In our judicial system, the court decides how long a person needs to remain in prison based upon the circumstances of the crime.

The Bible teaches that a person is not to be sentenced to death without the testimony of at least two witnesses. *Numbers 35:30 (NIV) ³⁰ "Anyone who kills a person is to be put to death as a murderer only on the testimony of witnesses. But no one is to be put to death on the testimony of only one witness.*
Can there be intentional taking of human life that is not considered murder? Yes. There is much bloodshed recorded in the Bible. Many people intentionally took the lives of others and were still considered innocent.

David took the lives of many. Yet God said that David was a man *after his own heart.* In fact, women

made up a song to praise him for it. *I Samuel 18:6-7 (NIV)* ⁶ *When the men were returning home after David had killed the Philistine, the women came out from all the towns of Israel to meet King Saul with singing and dancing, with joyful songs and with tambourines and lutes.* ⁷ *As they danced, they sang: "Saul has slain his thousands, and David his tens of thousands."*
Do you think it was murder when David killed Goliath? Of course not. All killing is not murder. Self-defense is a justifiable act. If all killing was murder, there would be no police enforcement, military rule, or other acts of self-defense. Notice this passage in "*Exodus 22:2-3 (NIV)* ² *"If a thief is caught breaking in and is struck so that he dies, the defender is not guilty of bloodshed;* ³ *but if it happens after sunrise, he is guilty of bloodshed. "A thief must certainly make restitution, but if he has nothing, he must be sold to pay for his theft."*

If a thief breaks into your house and you kill the thief, you are not guilty if it is done in the darkness. You would not have to go to the city of refuge for defending your property and your family. But if it is daylight, and you kill the defenseless thief, you would be guilty. These types of laws still apply today in our own judicial system.

The Hebrew definition of murder is the best description of murder in the eyes of God. The Hebrew word means, *"violent and unauthorized killing."* Hostility, anger, and hatred leads to this type of killing. The Hebrew word for murder is never used in the Bible for the execution of criminals or the killing of enemies of war. The word *authorized* is very important. Who gets to decide what is authorized killing and what is not? God's Word gives us the parameters to follow.

The Bible tells us in Romans to respect and obey government authority. God gives the government the authority to punish with the sword those who disobey. *Romans 13:4 (NIV) ⁴ For he is God's servant to do you good. But if you do wrong, be afraid, for he does not bear the sword for nothing. He is God's servant, an agent of wrath to bring punishment on the wrongdoer.*

The phrase *using the sword* refers to decapitating a criminal. Scripture describes those with God-given authority as *"agents of wrath."* God has given the government the right to administer capital punishment (the death penalty) to those who intentionally murder others. This type of killing is not murder, or God would be leading governments to sin, something He is incapable of doing.

The people in Nehemiah's time began to rebuild the wall as their opposition was rising. They prepared themselves for self-defense. *Nehemiah 4:16-18 (NIV) ¹⁶ From that day on, half of my men did the work, while the other half were equipped with spears, shields, bows and armor. The officers posted themselves behind all the people of Judah ¹⁷ who were building the wall. Those who carried materials did their work with one hand and held a weapon in the other, ¹⁸ and each of the builders wore his sword at his side as he worked. But the man who sounded the trumpet stayed with me.*

In Genesis, Chapter 14, Abraham defeated the tyrannical kings who captured his nephew, Lot, and others. It does not say specifically that there was bloodshed. However, we can assume that there was a battle because the word *defeated* alludes to the fact that men were killed in order to free the people.

Do you think that Hitler would have stopped killing just by being asked? Tyrants don't lay down their weapons and their power because they're asked to. Tyrants don't stop unless there is force and bloodshed. There are times when self-defense and standing up for others is necessary. Jesus said in *Luke 22:36 (NIV)* [36] *He said to them, "But now if you have a purse, take it, and also a bag; and if you don't have a sword, sell your cloak and buy one.*

There is a movement within our nation to revise history; to hide and discredit the events which unfolded during the formation of America. Our founders were God-fearing men who knew that religion and morality were indispensable for a nation to be free. These men were ready to defend the rights of the American people and stand up against the tyrannical rule of Great Britain.

People have tried to minimize the courage it took for our founding fathers to sign the Declaration of Independence. Some have even said that they were persecuted only because they were fighting against the government of the time. However, these men knew exactly what was at stake if they signed the Declaration; and they signed it anyway. The fight began with their signatures. They knew that there were British forces in their land and that Great Britain would most likely send more soldiers to regain control.

Many people today don't even know about the sufferings that were endured to free our nation. George Walton was wounded and captured as a prisoner of war. In 1778, Thomas Heyward Jr., Arthur Middleton, and Edward Rutledge were all captured in Savannah as they fought for our freedom.

Richard Stockton, of New Jersey, was dragged from his bed in the middle of the night and thrown into prison because he signed the Declaration of Independence. Many of the signers had their homes and property ransacked, looted, and vandalized by British soldiers and their followers. John Witherspoon, also of New Jersey, saw his eldest son, James, killed in the Battle of Germantown, in October, 1777.

Thomas McKean wrote to John Adams, in 1777, that he was *"hunted like a fox by the enemy, compelled to move family five times in three months, and had at last fixed them in a little log-house on the banks of the Susquehanna."*

Francis Lewis, while in Philadelphia attending to Congressional matters, had his home raided by the British and his wife taken as prisoner. She died shortly after her release. John Heart had his home vandalized and looted. He spent about a year on the run living in mountains, forests, and caves.

Phillip Livingston lost several of his properties to the British. He sold other properties to raise money for the war. He died in 1778. Lewis Morris lost his home, in 1776, to the British. They also took his livestock and horses. They eventually burned his property after looting it.

These men fought for our freedoms and took a stand against Great Britain. Some of them killed men to defend the freedoms that we now have. They established the second amendment which states, "*A well-regulated Militia, being necessary to the security of a free State, the right of the people to keep and bear Arms, shall not be infringed.*" The word militia means a body of citizens organized for military service.

Pastor Jonas Clark and the Minutemen were part of "*the shot heard 'round the world*"; the first battle of the American Revolution in 1775. Eight hundred British soldiers came to seize ammunition and guns and to take John Hancock and Sam Adams into custody. The British knew they could most likely find them at Pastor Jonas Clark's house. Pastor Clark had been preaching for years about tyranny, liberty, and self-defense. He had written many sermons and articles on the oppression of Britain and God's desire for man to be free.

Many of the Minutemen were from his church. These men decided to take a stand against the tyrannical rule of Britain and defend their property and land. There were about 100 of them. The terms militia and Minutemen are used interchangeably in many writings. Minutemen provided a highly mobile, rapidly deployed force that allowed the colonies to respond immediately to war threats, hence the name. The 100 men or so fought the 800 British. Eight minutemen died. The Minutemen had been trained by Pastor Clark for years. They could not instigate the war, but they could defend the land from the tyrant when necessary. The Minutemen stood almost motionless until the British fired first.

There is a memorial stone at the battle ground that reads, "*April 19, 1775. Stand your ground. Don't fire unless fired upon, but if they mean to have a war let it begin here.*"

Someone asked Pastor Clark prior to the battle if his men were ready to fight. Pastor Clark said, "*Yes, I have trained them for this very hour.*" As word spread that the British were attacking Americans, men from all over took up arms and defended their land and their families.

Recorded sermons from these times speak of a Biblical self-defense and help explain why Americans acted as they did. They were being oppressed by Great Britain and felt a just cause to stand against the tyranny.

This excerpt is from a sermon titled *Arising and Pleading His Peoples Cause* by Abraham Keteltas. He stated, "*Every engine has been employed to ruin our commerce, trade, husbandry and religion: Every method has been contrived and executed, to deprive us of the necessaries of life, and cause us to perish for the want of food, clothing, and the means of defense. Our ships have been seized and confiscated, our poor brethren, taken in them, compelled to fight against us: our prisoners starved to death; our wives and daughters have been ravished: numerous families of little ones compelled to leave their own habitations and provisions, wander about in a strange land, beg their bread, and expose themselves to all the severity of the season.*" (Ellis Sandoz, *Political Sermons of the American Founding Era: 1730-1805*, 2 Vol. Foreword by Ellis Sandoz (2nd ed. Indianapolis: Liberty Fund, 1998). Vol. 1. Chapter: *19: Abraham Keteltas, GOD ARISING AND PLEADING HIS PEOPLE'S CAUSE* Accessed from http://oll.libertyfund.org/title/816/69274/1668599 on 2014-02-21)

John Allen wrote a sermon titled *An Oration Upon the Beauties of Liberty*. Allen said, "But God forbid that I should be thought to aim at rousing the Americans to arms, without their rights, liberties and oppression call for it. For they are unwilling to beat to arms, they are loyal subjects; they love their king; they love their mother-

country; they call it their home; and with nothing more than the prosperity of Britain, and the glory of their king: But they will not give up their rights; they will not be slaves to any power upon earth. Therefore, my Lord, as a peace-maker; as their agent; as their friend; lay their grievances before their king. Let the Americans enjoy their birthright blessings, and Britain her prosperity, let there be a mutual union between the mother and her children, in all the blessings of life, trade and happiness; then, my Lord, both Britons, and Americans, will call you blessed." (Ellis Sandoz, *Political Sermons of the American Founding Era: 1730-1805*, 2 Vol. Foreword by Ellis Sandoz (2nd ed. Indianapolis: Liberty Fund, 1998). Vol. I. Chapter: 10: John Allen, AN ORATION UPON THE BEAUTIES OF LIBERTY Accessed from http://oll.libertyfund.org/title/816/69240/1668020 on 2014-02-21)

We need to understand that Satan is the one influencing tyrants to do such evil. We are to love our enemies and pray for those who persecute us. This doesn't mean that we shouldn't defend our rights or defend our land. Jesus goes to the heart of the matter and teaches us further about the command not to murder in *Matthew 5:21-26 (NIV)* [21] *"You have heard that it was said to the people long ago, 'Do not murder, and anyone who murders will be subject to judgment.'* [22] *But I tell you that anyone who is angry with his brother will be subject to judgment. Again, anyone who says to his brother, 'Raca,' is answerable to the Sanhedrin. But anyone who says, 'You fool!' will be in danger of the fire of hell.*

If we are angry with our brother, then we are missing God's heart of love. God did not create man to do heinous acts. He did not create man to rape, murder, and steal. Just like He did not create Adolf Hitler to commit evil in this world. He created him to glorify and serve Him, but Hitler made the choice to follow Satan and carry out his wishes instead. The following passages reveal Satan's influence in people's lives. *I John 5:19 (NIV) [19] We know that we are children of God, and that the whole world is under the control of the evil one. John 10:10 (NIV) [10] The thief comes only to steal and kill and destroy; I have come that they may have life, and have it to the full.*

The Bible says in *I Timothy 2:1-4 (NIV) [1] I urge, then, first of all, that requests, prayers, intercession and thanksgiving be made for everyone— [2] for kings and all those in authority, that we may live peaceful and quiet lives in all godliness and holiness. [3] This is good, and pleases God our Savior, [4] who wants all men to be saved and to come to a knowledge of the truth.*
Did God want people to pray for Hitler during his time of authority? Yes. It is God's desire for all to know Him. We are commanded to love our enemies. We know that it is only by God's grace that we are saved.

God's judgment resides with the heart on cases of murder. The Bible tells us Jesus sees the heart. Jesus elevated the consequences of murder from the physical act to a heart that hates someone. Have you called someone a fool? Do you think such thoughts in your head? Have you scowled at someone, rolled your eyes, or said harsh words with a hateful intent? Are you guilty of a heart that commits murder? There are times when we do not need to defend ourselves. We need to be willing to be persecuted for Christ. All of the Apostles were tortured for their faith. All but one was murdered for their faith. Have you ever wondered why they didn't defend themselves?

Jesus said in Matthew 5:38-42 (NIV) [38] "You have heard that it was said, 'Eye for eye, and tooth for tooth.' [39] But I tell you, Do not resist an evil person. If someone strikes you on the right cheek, turn to him the other also. [40] And if someone wants to sue you and take your tunic, let him have your cloak as well. [41] If someone forces you to go one mile, go with him two miles. [42] Give to the one who asks you, and do not turn away from the one who wants to borrow from you.

I Peter 3:14 (NIV) [14] But even if you should suffer for what is right, you are blessed. "Do not fear what they fear; do not be frightened."

We are told to set the oppressed free and to defend the rights of others. However, we are also told that we are blessed if we are persecuted and suffer for the glory of Christ. *Psalm 82:3-4 (NIV) [3] Defend the cause of the weak and fatherless; maintain the rights of the poor and oppressed. [4] Rescue the weak and needy; deliver them from the hand of the wicked.*

Jeremiah 21:12 (NIV) ¹² *O house of David, this is what the LORD says: "'Administer justice every morning; rescue from the hand of his oppressor the one who has been robbed, or my wrath will break out and burn like fire because of the evil you have done– burn with no one to quench it.*

Proverbs 24:11,12 (NIV) ¹¹ *Rescue those being led away to death; hold back those staggering toward slaughter.* ¹² *If you say, "But we knew nothing about this," does not he who weighs the heart perceive it? Does not he who guards your life know it? Will he not repay each person according to what he has done?*

Do you remember when David killed Goliath? The Bible says in *I Samuel 17:1-2 (NIV)* ¹ Now **the Philistines gathered their forces for war** and *assembled at Socoh in Judah. They pitched camp at Ephes Dammim, between Socoh and Azekah.* The Philistines gathered their forces for war so they could oppress the Israelities.² *Saul and the Israelites assembled and camped in the Valley of Elah and* **drew up their battle line to meet the Philistines**. The Israelites gathered to defend themselves. The Bible says that David killed Goliath. It does not say that he murdered him. *I Samuel 17:45 (NIV)* ⁴⁵ *David said to the Philistine, "You come against me with sword and spear and javelin, but I come against you in the name of the LORD Almighty, the God of the armies of Israel, whom you have defied.*

We need to pray and search God's Word to know when to defend ourselves or set the oppressed free. We need to self-govern; learn to forgive one another; and move away from hating each other. Hostility and hatred only destroys a nation. We must learn God's principles and apply them to our lives, if we want to live in a land that is peaceful and free.

WORKSHEET FOR CIVIL GOVERNMENT
LIFE TRUTH # 6
YOU SHALL NOT MURDER

Question: What does it mean to murder?
Answer: Murder is the unauthorized and intentional killing of a human life.

Exodus 20:13 (NIV) [13] *"You shall not murder.*

> Write out the Life Truth, question, and answer on one side of an index card and the verse on the other side. Keep it in your Bible for the week. Work on it every day individually and as a family. Have it memorized by next week.

Read Genesis 6:5-13. The people had become corrupt and V_____. (v 11,13)

Read Genesis 9:5,6. What did God require of men after the flood?

Why is this phrase important in not murdering others? *"for in the image of God has God made man."* Our military uses video games to prepare men into being ready to fight and kill. Similar games can now be purchased for anyone to play. Explain why or why not this is good for a society?

Every life that God creates is precious and should be valued. How is our society becoming more and more violent and not respecting life?

Read Exodus 21:12-14. God instituted the death penalty. In this passage, what key word deserves the death penalty and finds the person guilty of murder?

Can you think of a passage in the Bible where killing was justifiable? If so, what was it?

Read I Samuel 14:45-51. Would you consider this murder? Why or why not?

Read Matt. 5:21-26. Jesus elevated the judgment of murder from the physical act to what?

Read Matt. 5:43-48. Should we be angry about what Hitler did? Should we hate Hitler? What's the difference?

Here are two Biblical teachings; defend the oppressed and suffer for doing right. Write down which teaching these passages refer to.
Prov. 24:11,12　　　　　　Matt. 5:38-42
Luke 22:36　　　　　　　I Peter 3:17

How could returning to teaching The Ten Commandments, specifically this command, help our society?

Based on this LIFE TRUTH, is there any anger in your heart that needs to be dealt with so that you will not be guilty of murder? How can you help others understand justifiable killing?

CIVIL GOVERNMENT
LIFE TRUTH # 7
YOU SHALL NOT COMMIT ADULTERY

There is a debate about civil rights in our nation today. The word *civil* means "of or relating to citizens." Civil rights are the rights and privileges of citizens; the freedoms and liberties that we should possess.

Some think that old-fashioned views are harming our current civil rights. What are these old-fashioned views? In 1824, in the case of Updegraph v. The Commonwealth, the Pennsylvania Supreme Court declared, *"The act against cursing and swearing, and breach of the Lord's Day; the act forbidding incestuous marriages, perjury by taking a false oath upon the book, fornication and adultery…for all these are founded in Christianity – for all these are restraints upon civil liberty."* Until the 1960's, this nation supported restraints upon civil liberty and punished those who broke them. Today, not only are there are no serious consequences for these restraints, but adultery and fornication are barely even scoffed at as sin. The founding fathers wrote our laws based upon Christian morals. They understood that there needed to be consequences when laws were broken. In the Old Testament, the consequence for adultery was the death penalty. Leviticus 20:10 (NIV) [10] *"'If a man commits adultery with another man's wife—with the wife of his neighbor—both the adulterer and the adulteress must be put to death.* God established these laws for our protection. Adultery is a sin that destroys a nation. It destroys marriages, families, and societies. In 1898, the Washington Supreme Court stated, *"Adultery, whether promiscuous or not, violates one of the Ten Commandments and the statutes of this state."* What has happened to the commitment to the Ten Commandments as the basis for laws in our nation? We are seeing the moral decay right before our eyes. We have slipped away from God and His truth by deciding to do what is right in our own eyes. We have turned away from the Bible as the only authority.

Our nation is suffering from this pattern of destructive behavior. We are sliding down the slippery slope of indifference. We are no longer offended by sin. Adultery has become a non-issue in our world. Same sex marriage is viewed as a civil right and has been legalized in some states. And sadly, we haven't even reached the bottom of this slope of destruction. You can be sure that more and more perversions will invade society when the Bible is no longer the standard as to what is right and what is wrong.

Is our path of destruction really that bad? Yes! Look at society today. We have dropped the ball on punishing adultery. Our neighborhoods are full of confused, broken, hurting, depressed, addicted, lonely, and unmotivated people. Broken parents pass on their scars to the next generation. Our world is crumbling as God's moral compass is being broken. God gave us His laws as warning signs for our own protection and benefit. *You shall not commit adultery.* There are people in this generation who are fighting for the civil rights of homosexuals. They tell those who are opposed to legalizing homosexuality that they are on the wrong side of history. Their argument is based upon the history of slavery; how at one time black people were oppressed in this nation until the realization that all men are created equal. They believe that one day we will look back and say, *"I can't believe we oppressed the homosexuals just like we oppressed the blacks."*

Are they right? Will we look back and say such a thing? Will legalizing homosexual marriages benefit society? **Absolutely NOT!** Were we right to free the blacks and defend their civil rights? **Absolutely YES!** It was right for us to stand up for the oppressed and help them gain their freedom. But there is a huge difference between the two. The Bible is clear that we are all equal in God's eyes. We all deserve the freedom that God intended for us to have. We are all made in the image of God. No one is to be treated with less dignity than anyone else. Colossians 3:11 (NIV)[11] *Here there is no Greek or Jew, circumcised or uncircumcised, barbarian, Scythian, slave or free, but Christ is all, and is in all.*

Since this is true with our ethnicity, can this also be true of our sexual preferences? NO. Freedom of homosexuality is against Scripture. God is for our civil rights, but He condemns this type of relationship. The Bible never contradicts itself. It condemns homosexuality. It speaks of homosexuality as a wicked act.

I Corinthians 6:9-11 (NIV) [9] Do you not know that the wicked will not inherit the kingdom of God? Do not be deceived: Neither the sexually immoral nor idolaters nor adulterers nor male prostitutes nor homosexual offenders [10] nor thieves nor the greedy nor drunkards nor slanderers nor swindlers will inherit the kingdom of God. [11] And that is what some of you were. But you were washed, you were sanctified, you were justified in the name of the Lord Jesus Christ and by the Spirit of our God.

Notice that it lists several other things that are considered wicked; one of them being adultery. If we are going to use the Bible as our guidebook, then we need to obey all of it. Fornication, or *sexual immorality,* is a criminal act. Notice the seriousness of the judgment upon these wicked people, "They will not inherit the kingdom of God." There should be consequences here upon the earth, but the greatest consequence will be for those who do not repent of these sins. The Bible says that they will not enter the kingdom of heaven.

Look around at the pain in people's eyes. Much of it is due to relationship failures. People have been cheated upon, lied to, stolen from, and left for another. Many children have been raised with the absence of a parent. God's design is for one man and one woman to come together until death they do part.

We are to be people of our word. We are to keep our commitments before God. Here is a traditional wedding vow: *I_____ , take you _____, to be my lawfully wedded wife, to have and to hold, from this day forward, for better, for worse, for richer, for poorer, in sickness and in health, to love and to cherish, till death do us part, and hereto I pledge to you my faithfulness.*

Traditional vows are still the most popular. Some vows today may differ on a phrase or two, but most of them have this meaning and commitment. When we marry, are we ready to keep this covenant with our spouse? Are we ready to keep it before the God that we have asked to consecrate our union?

If our laws today still discouraged adultery and punished evildoers, more people would think twice about cheating on their spouse. Couples would work harder at reconciliation and forgiveness. If you speed down the highway and no one stops you, before too long many will be speeding down the highway making the road very dangerous. We need civil restraints in our laws to keep us from harming ourselves. These restraints are written in God's Word. *You shall not...* It is a proven fact that children are healthier when they are raised in stable homes that have one father and one mother. It is not an ideal environment for children to have two moms and two dads due to the unfaithfulness of their birthparents. God has a perfect design for the family. We need to live by His principles and bring honor to this God-ordained institution.

Civil government is responsible to protect society from moral decay. It should punish moral crimes when they are committed. Adultery is a crime. The word crime means an act or the commission of an act that is forbidden. God forbade sexual immorality when he said, *"You shall not commit adultery."*

In 1889, the United States Supreme Court ruled in the case of Davis v. Beason. Samuel Davis was caught in the crime of bigamy and polygamy. He was fined and jailed for his actions. His defense was the first amendment. He said that his "religious beliefs" were in favor of polygamy. Davis believed that he should be free to have these types of relationships. Justice Stephen Field, who was appointed by Abraham Lincoln, read the Supreme Court's ruling on this matter. *"Bigamy and polygamy are crimes by the laws of all civilized and Christian countries. They are crimes by the laws of the United States, and they are crimes by the laws of Idaho. They tend to destroy the purity of the marriage relation, to disturb the peace of families…To extend exemption from punishment for such crimes would be to shock the moral judgment of the community. To call their advocacy a tenet of religion is to offend the commons sense of mankind…The constitutions of several states, in providing for religious freedom, have declared expressly that such freedom shall not be construed to excuse acts of licentiousness."*

Licentiousness is the lack of moral restraint regarding sexual relations.

You cannot suggest that you are doing something based upon your own "religious beliefs." A nation needs a standard by which to judge their morals. We used to cherish the Bible. God's Word was the standard by which we lived. The current generation is moving away from the belief that Scripture should be the basis for our laws. Even conservative groups are beginning to think we need to protect all religious beliefs and theories. Once we open up the door to all religions, we will have men like Samuel David claiming they can do immoral acts based upon their own religious beliefs.

Our laws on adultery have become lax. Is it right for Christians to stand against homosexual relationships but allow fornication and adultery? No! All are considered wicked acts according to the Word of God. All should have a civil consequence based upon the severity of the crime. Do we think thieves should be punished? Do we think liars should be punished? Do we think murderers should be punished?

In the Old Testament, fornication was a criminal offense. Deuteronomy 22:20-21 (NIV) [20] *If, however, the charge is true and no proof of the girl's virginity can* be found, [21] she shall be brought to the door of her father's house and there the men of her town shall stone her to death. She has done a disgraceful thing in Israel by being promiscuous while still in her father's house. You must purge the evil from among you. In our generation, it is not considered a sin to have sex before you are married, even in the church.

On January 30, 1905, in a message to Congress, President Theodore Roosevelt stated, *"The institution of marriage is, of course, at the very foundation of our social organization, and all influences that affect that institution are of vital concern to the people of the whole country. There is a widespread concern that the divorce laws are dangerously lax and indifferently administered in some of the states, resulting in the diminishing regard for the sanctity of the marriage relation. The hope is entertained that co-operation amongst the several states can be secured to the end that there may be enacted upon the subject of marriage and divorce uniform laws, containing all possible safeguards for the security of the family."*

People need to be taught what God's Word says. They need to know what is morally acceptable to God and what is not. The church has become Biblically illiterate. We have become lax in our convictions and standards. Our mission is to share the gospel! We are to make disciples! Do you believe in Jesus and what He has done for you? Then speak up for Him and His Word! Teach people what is moral and what is immoral based on God's Word.

I must admit that I have two loves in my life. My first love is not my wife, Christy. If you were to ask her, I'm sure that she would tell you that I am not her first love either. Both of us have the same first love. We are both engaged to Christ and look forward to our wedding day with Him when He returns. This is, of course, symbolic but it illustrates how intimate our spiritual relationship with Christ should be. The church is called "*the bride of Christ.*" We are to keep ourselves fully devoted to Him. God is to be our first love as the first commandment states, "*You shall have no other gods (or loves) before me.*"

When Paul wrote to the church at Corinth, he reminded them of the passion and devotion they should have with Christ and Christ alone. *2 Corinthians 11:2-3 (NIV) [2] I am jealous for you with a godly jealousy. I promised you to one husband, to Christ, so that I might present you as a pure virgin to him. [3] But I am afraid that just as Eve was deceived by the serpent's cunning, your minds may somehow be led astray from your sincere and pure devotion to Christ.*

Paul warned them of the many false religions and teachings that could lead people away from their devotion to Christ and His Word. In the first four commandments of the Ten Commandments, we learned that our devotion should be solely to God. If God is our first love, then we are going to do all we can to get to know him and to please Him. Just like when two people love each other. They begin to study one another. They want to know everything about each other. They want to please the person that they love.

When we begin to slip away from our relationship to Him, the signs become obvious. The same thing happens when a marriage falls apart. Signs of intimacy between a husband and wife begin to fade. It is evident on their faces, in their actions, and in their devotion to one another. The passion to please the other is lost. The *"I don't care what you think"* attitude arises.

This type of attitude toward God is called spiritual adultery. Look at what is says in *Jeremiah 3:6 (NIV)* *⁶ During the reign of King Josiah, the LORD said to me, "Have you seen what faithless Israel has done? She has gone up on every high hill and under every spreading tree and has committed adultery there.* Jeremiah is talking about the nation of Israel. They left their first love and chased after other loves; the loves of this world. They spent more time getting to know the pleasures of the world, than they did getting to know God and His Word. They were called faithless because their loyalty to God and His laws was pushed aside and unimportant. They felt that obeying God's law was unnecessary and a burden to them.

Our nation is becoming like a faithless Israel. People say we are on the wrong side of history if we do not support the civil rights of homosexuals. If people really knew their history, they would know a nation that becomes faithless to God suffers consequences.

Just look at Sodom and Gomorrah; they were in favor of homosexual relationships and it eventually destroyed them.

The amazing thing about God is that no matter what we do, He still longs for us to restore a relationship with Him. But we must repent and return to Him with all of our hearts. We must be committed to all Ten Commandments and the teachings of Christ. God is as equally upset by homosexual offenders, as He is adulterers, and Sabbath breakers.

Jeremiah 3:8-13 (NIV) [8] I gave faithless Israel her certificate of divorce and sent her away because of all her adulteries. Yet I saw that her unfaithful sister Judah had no fear; she also went out and committed adultery. [9] Because Israel's immorality mattered so little to her, she defiled the land and committed adultery with stone and wood. [10] In spite of all this, her unfaithful sister **Judah did not return to me with all her heart**, but only in pretense," declares the LORD. [11] The LORD said to me, "Faithless Israel is more righteous than unfaithful Judah. [12] Go, proclaim this message toward the north: "'Return, faithless Israel,' declares the LORD, 'I will frown on you no longer, for I am merciful,' declares the LORD, 'I will not be angry forever. [13] **<u>Only acknowledge your guilt-- you have rebelled against the LORD your God</u>**, you have scattered your favors to foreign gods under every spreading tree, and have not obeyed me,'" declares the LORD.

When we become lax in our morals of fornication and adultery, we are basically saying to God, "Your standards are a little too harsh. We want to be able to enjoy ourselves and seek after our pleasures." Unfortunately, our lax morals are destroying the strong nation we once had. God will punish and curse nations that turn against Him. *Jeremiah 23:10-15 (NIV) [10] The land is full of adulterers;* **because of the curse** *the land lies parched and the pastures in the desert are withered. The [prophets] follow an evil course and use their power unjustly. [11] "Both prophet and priest are godless; even in my temple I find their wickedness," declares the LORD. [12] "Therefore their path will become slippery;* **they will be banished** *to darkness and there they will fall.* **I will bring disaster on them in the year they are punished***," declares the LORD.*
[13] "Among the prophets of Samaria I saw this repulsive thing: They prophesied by Baal and led my people Israel astray. [14] And among the prophets of Jerusalem I have seen something horrible: They commit adultery and live a lie. They strengthen the hands of evildoers, so that no one turns from his wickedness. They are all like Sodom to me; the people of Jerusalem are like Gomorrah." [15] Therefore, this is what the LORD Almighty says concerning the prophets: "I will make them eat bitter food and drink poisoned water, because from the prophets of Jerusalem ungodliness has spread throughout the land."

After the Civil War, Abraham Lincoln issued a proclamation calling the nation to repent and to confess their sins. Oppressing the blacks was a sin.

Lincoln felt that the war was God's judgment upon the nation.

By the President of the United States of America
A Proclamation

Whereas the Senate of the United States, devoutly recognizing the supreme authority and just government of Almighty God in all the affairs of men and of nations, has by a resolution requested the President to designate and set apart a day for national prayer and humiliation; and

Whereas it is the duty of nations as well as of men to own their dependence upon the overruling power of God, to confess their sins and transgressions in humble sorrow, yet with assured hope that genuine repentance will lead to mercy and pardon, and to recognize the sublime truth, announced in the Holy Scriptures and proven by all history, that those nations only are blessed whose God is the Lord;

And, insomuch as we know that by His divine law nations, like individuals, are subjected to punishments and chastisements in this world, <u>may we not justly fear that the awful calamity of civil war which now desolates the land may be but a punishment inflicted upon us for our presumptuous sins</u>, to the needful end of our national reformation as a whole people? We have been the recipients of the choicest bounties of Heaven; we have been preserved these many years in peace and prosperity; we have grown in numbers, wealth, and power as no other nation has ever grown. But we have forgotten God.

We have forgotten the gracious hand which preserved us in peace and multiplied and enriched and strengthened us, and we have vainly imagined, in the deceitfulness of our hearts, that all these blessings were produced by some superior wisdom and virtue of our own. Intoxicated with unbroken success, we have become too self-sufficient to feel the necessity of redeeming and preserving grace, too proud to pray to the God that made us.

<u>*It behooves us, then, to humble ourselves before the offended Power, to confess our national sins, and to pray for clemency and forgiveness.*</u>

Now, therefore, in compliance with the request, and fully concurring in the views of the Senate, I do by this my proclamation designate and set apart Thursday, the 30th day of April, 1863, as a day of national humiliation, fasting, and prayer. And I do hereby request all the people to abstain on that day from their ordinary secular pursuits, and to unite at their several places of public worship and their respective homes in keeping the day holy to the Lord and devoted to the humble discharge of the religious duties proper to that solemn occasion.

All this being done in sincerity and truth, let us then rest humbly in the hope authorized by the divine teachings that the united cry of the nation will be heard on high and answered with blessings no less than the pardon of our national sins and the restoration of our now divided and suffering country to its former happy condition of unity and peace. In witness whereof I have hereunto set my hand and caused the seal of the United States to be affixed.

Done at the city of Washington, this 30th day of March, A. D. 1863, and of the Independence of the United States the eighty-seventh.

If we legalize homosexuality, we will be offending God. We will be going against His moral standards for relationships according to His Holy Word. We will be bringing judgment upon ourselves. We will not be moving forward in history. We will be repeating a terrible mistake that other societies have made before us. We must return to God's Holy Word for our standards. We must begin being a "faithful" America again: A Christian nation that is committed to Christian principles. We must punish moral crimes listed in God's Word.

The Biblical family is almost dead in our society. It must be resurrected. Fathers must be spiritual leaders in their homes, first by example, and then by teaching others. Parents must put God and His Word first in their lives. Families need to read the Bible together, pray together, praise together, and seek Christ together. Families need to learn the Biblical institutions (Self / Family / Church / Civil) and begin rebuilding a godly society. Our civilization depends on it. We need to humble ourselves, fast, and pray for our nation; just as Abraham Lincoln proclaimed years ago. If God can revive this nation from a civil war, He can do it again. But we must return to Him.

Adultery lives in the heart; just as murder lives in the heart before the act is committed. *Mark 7:21 (NIV) 21 For from within, out of men's hearts, come evil thoughts, sexual immorality, theft, murder, adultery.* We must be very cautious about being angry with our brother, because anger leads to hate, and hate can eventually lead to murder. Jesus said that if we allow our heart to hate our brother, we are as guilty as a murderer. The same is true with lust. If we lust in our hearts, we are as guilty as an adulterer.

Matthew 5:27-30 (NIV) 27 "You have heard that it was said, 'Do not commit adultery.' 28 But I tell you that anyone who looks at a woman lustfully has already committed adultery with her in his heart. 29 If your right eye causes you to sin, gouge it out and throw it away. It is better for you to lose one part of your body than for your whole body to be thrown into hell. 30 And if your right hand causes you to sin, cut it off and throw it away. It is better for you to lose one part of your body than for your whole body to go into hell.

Lusting means that we look at someone with the intent of being with them intimately. The first glance is not the danger. It is the second look and the gazing that becomes the danger. The heart can be deceitful and full of selfish evil. If not controlled, it is capable of many hurtful acts.

Men and women who commit adultery begin by doing it in their hearts and minds. It becomes a premeditated offense. It is an emotional relationship with another person until passion gives way and the act is committed. People commit physical adultery, emotional adultery, and spiritual adultery. All are sinful in the eyes of God. All must be guarded against.

Jesus warns us about committing these sins in our hearts. Lust opens the door for Satan to bring in perversions and crimes against others. Today's society glorifies pornography, promiscuity, adultery, and homosexuality. The Bible says in *Proverbs 5:18-23 (NIV)* *[18] May your fountain be blessed, and may you rejoice in the wife of your youth. [19] A loving doe, a graceful deer– may her breasts satisfy you always, may you ever be captivated by her love. [20] Why be captivated, my son, by an adulteress? Why embrace the bosom of another man's wife? [21] For a man's ways are in full view of the LORD, and he examines all his paths. [22] The evil deeds of a wicked man ensnare him; the cords of his sin hold him fast. [23] He will die for lack of discipline, led astray by his own great folly.*

Where is faithful America? Where have the faithful people gone? Our evil deeds ensnare us and the cords of our sin hold us fast. We will die for lack of discipline if we do not repent. Christ and Christ alone can save us. He enables us to walk in righteousness and self-control.

We can see America's future by reading what Paul wrote to the Romans. When we no longer think that God's laws are to be feared and obeyed, God will darken our minds and our society will suffer. Perversion will not stop with gay marriage. The ACLU is already fighting for trans-genders and bisexuals. Polygamy and other "civil rights" will be next.

Romans 1:21-32 (NIV) [21] For although they knew God, they neither glorified him as God nor gave thanks to him, but their thinking became futile and their foolish hearts were darkened. [22] Although they claimed to be wise, they became fools [23] and exchanged the glory of the immortal God for images made to look like mortal man and birds and animals and reptiles. [24] Therefore God gave them over in the sinful desires of their hearts to sexual impurity for the degrading of their bodies with one another. [25] They exchanged the truth of God for a lie, and worshiped and served created things rather than the Creator—who is forever praised. Amen. [26] Because of this, God gave them over to shameful lusts. Even their women exchanged natural relations for unnatural ones. [27] In the same way the men also abandoned natural relations with women and were inflamed with lust for one another. Men committed indecent acts with other men, and received in themselves the due penalty for their perversion. [28] Furthermore, since they did not think it worthwhile to retain the knowledge of God, he gave them over to a depraved mind, to do what ought not to be done. [29] They have become filled with every kind of wickedness, evil, greed and depravity. They are full of envy, murder, strife, deceit and malice. They are gossips, ³⁰ slanderers, God-haters, insolent, arrogant and boastful; they invent ways of doing evil; they disobey their parents; ³¹ they are senseless, faithless, heartless, ruthless. ³² Although they know God's righteous decree that those who do such things deserve death, they not only continue to do these very things but also approve of those who practice them.

Our only hope is to repent. We must repent individually, as families, as churches, and as a nation. Jeremiah 3:12-13 (NIV) ¹² Go, proclaim this message toward the north: "'Return, faithless Israel,' declares the LORD, 'I will frown on you no longer, for I am merciful,' declares the LORD, 'I will not be angry forever. ¹³ Only acknowledge your guilt– you have rebelled against the LORD your God, you have scattered your favors to foreign gods under every spreading tree, and have not obeyed me,'" declares the LORD.

If you are in an adulterous relationship, **get out of it.** If you are in a sexually immoral relationship, **get out of it.** If you are lusting in your heart, **repent.** Reconcile with your spouse. Stay committed to your spouse. Live as if fornication and adultery are criminal offenses...because they are! Judges may not punish you on this earth, but don't think you won't be punished on Judgment Day.

Romans 2:5-8 (NIV) ⁵ But because of your stubbornness and your unrepentant heart, you are storing up wrath against yourself for the day of God's wrath, when his righteous judgment will be revealed. ⁶ God "will give to *each person according to what he has done." ⁷ To those who by persistence in doing good seek glory, honor and immortality, he will give eternal life. ⁸ But for those who are self-seeking and who reject the truth and follow evil, there will be wrath and anger.*

An incident is recorded in the Bible where the Pharisee's arrested a woman caught in the act of adultery. They brought her before Jesus. Her accuser's had stones in their hands and were ready to kill her. Jesus had a different idea. He saw the woman's heart.

John 8:7-11 (NIV) ⁷ When they kept on questioning him, he straightened up and said to them, "If any one of you is without sin, let him be the first to throw a stone at her." ⁸ Again he stooped down and wrote on the ground. ⁹ At this, those who heard began to go away one at a time, the older ones first, until only Jesus was left, with the woman still standing there. ¹⁰ Jesus straightened up and asked her, "Woman, where are they? Has no one condemned you?" ¹¹ "No one, sir," she said. "Then neither do I condemn you," Jesus declared. "Go now and leave your life of sin."

How awesome it must have felt to hear these words from Christ: *"Then neither do I condemn you."* Jesus knew that this woman was filled with shame, guilt, and remorse. He knew that judgment was not what she needed. She needed grace and mercy.

Jesus welcomes the heart of a remorseful, broken sinner. But being remorseful for the sin is not enough. We must repent and turn away from our criminal behavior. Don't miss His closing declaration! Jesus declared, *"Go now and leave your life of sin."*

WORKSHEET FOR CIVIL GOVERNMENT
LIFE TRUTH # 7
YOU SHALL NOT COMMIT ADULTERY

Question: What does it mean to commit adultery?
Answer: Adultery is the crime of unfaithfulness to your spouse.

Exodus 20:14 (NIV) [14] *"You shall not commit adultery.*

> Write out the Life Truth, question, and answer on one side of an index card and the verse on the other side. Keep it in your Bible for the week. Work on it every day individually and as a family. Have it memorized by next week.

Read Hebrews 13:4 What will happen to all the adulterers and the sexually immoral?

How can you honor marriage even before you are married?

Healthy Biblical families produce healthy societies. In what ways have you seen adultery, divorce, and fornication negatively affect our society?

What types of emotional issues do these sins bring upon children?

Read 1 Thess. 4:3-8. How is adultery and sexual immorality harming our brother?

Read Proverbs 6:32. What will happen to the adulterer?

Read Proverbs, Chapter 5. List a few things that we can learn from this chapter.

What kinds of temptations, in our generation, are leading people to commit adultery?

Read Luke 16:18. How could this verse help benefit our society?

Read Matthew 5:27-30. What have you committed when you lust?

Does Jesus really want us to gouge out an eye? Why or why not?

Is lusting a serious sin? What are the consequences based on this passage?

Read 1 Cor. 6:9-10. List two other wicked sins deserving of hell.

Read John 8:1-11. Is Jesus willing to forgive those who have committed adultery? What does He require of them? (V 11)

Based on this LIFE TRUTH, how can you be faithful to the marriage bed? How can you help others understand the dangers of adultery?

CIVIL GOVERNMENT
LIFE TRUTH # 8
YOU SHALL NOT STEAL

The definition of *steal* in Webster's Dictionary is *to take the property of another wrongfully, especially as a habitual or regular practice.* Stealing is a criminal offense. When someone takes something that does not belong to them or that they have not earned it violates the rights of people to rule their own property. God's design is for people to be productive in society and to earn the bread that they eat. His plan is for people to own property and to enjoy the fruits of their labor.

In a free society based upon God's laws, people feel more trustworthy. They trust each other because of the laws of the land and the prohibitions that have been set in place to govern the nation. In this country, at one time, people actually slept with their doors unlocked. They left their cars unlocked with the keys inside. They trusted their neighbors as well as those in the communities around them.
It is God's desire that we live in freedom and that no man rules harshly over another. The key to such a society is in making the Lord our God.

Psalm 33:12 (NIV) ^{12} Blessed is the nation whose God is the LORD.

God took the nation of Israel out of a land of slavery and into a land flowing with milk and honey. The phrase *milk and honey* is about abundance and provisions. God desires to provide for the nation who obeys Him and makes Him their Lord. God's provisions enable them to bless other nations with the surplus of His bounty.

Deuteronomy 28:12-13 (NIV) [12] *The LORD will open the heavens, the storehouse of his bounty, to send rain on your land in season and to bless all the work of your hands. You will lend to many nations but will borrow from none.* [13] *The LORD will make you the head, not the tail. If you pay attention to the commands of the LORD your God that I give you this day and carefully follow them, you will always be at the top, never at the bottom.*

We are to use His provisions wisely. Genesis 1:26 (NIV) [26] *Then God said, "Let us make man in our image, in our likeness, and* **let them rule** *over the fish of the sea and the birds of the air, over the livestock, over all the earth, and over all the creatures that move along the ground."*

God has given us dominion over the land and everything in it. The word dominion means ruling. It is an authority that should not be abused. We are to rule over our own property and treat the property of others with great respect. God condemns those who take advantage of others. Leviticus 25:13-14,17 (NIV) [13] *"'In this Year of Jubilee everyone is to return to his own property.* [14] *"'If you sell land to one of your countrymen or buy any from him, do not take advantage of each other...* [17] *Do not take advantage of each other, but fear your God. I am the LORD your God.*

Stealing is a grave offense in God's eyes. It is a violation of a person's right to rule their own property. Stealing in the eyes of God is to manipulate for your own gain, cut corners for your own profit, and misuse your authority over others. God wants us to have full lives. Part of having a full life is the ability to rule or govern our own property. He has given us the right and freedom to use our property as we see fit for His glory. This includes being led by God to sell our possessions or use them to help the poor and needy.

It is vital to a free society that we raise our children to respect the property of others. If we abuse this freedom, we open doors to greater abuses. Wall Street has become a perfect example of how greedy people can abuse authority and steal from others. Robbery has also become a daily event throughout our land.

God has much to say in the Bible about stealing.

1. Don't steal someone's property

Deuteronomy 19:14 (NIV) [14] *Do not move your neighbor's boundary stone set up by your predecessors in the inheritance you receive in the land the LORD your*

God is giving you to possess. Deuteronomy 27:17 (NIV) ¹⁷ "Cursed is the man who moves his neighbor's boundary stone." Then all the people shall say, "Amen!"

The boundary stone was used by nations to mark property. People who became jealous or envious of another person's property would gradually move the boundary stone. They did it for selfish gain; to illegally acquire more property. God warned against taking the property of another.

2. Make money honestly

Proverbs 11:1 (NIV) ¹ The LORD abhors dishonest scales, but accurate weights are his delight. . He abhors costs that are higher than the items or labor is worth. He abhors dishonest scales that give sellers extra profits on each sale. God wants us to treat one another fairly and justly.

Proverbs 13:11 (NIV) ¹¹ Dishonest money dwindles away, but he who gathers money little by little makes it grow.

3. Remove all deception

Proverbs 20:17 (NIV) ¹⁷ Food gained by fraud tastes sweet to a man, but he ends up with a mouth full of gravel.

Casinos are excellent examples of deception. They promise people wealth, but in the end take their money. The idea of getting rich entices people into playing and then losing what they have. It is deceit and trickery; a very real type of fraud. We are not to deceive people in our business dealings. We are to always tell the truth. We are stealing when we use fraud as a means to gain wealth for ourselves. To know that a product is faulty, or not worth what it is being sold for, is fraud. *Get rich quick* schemes or *pyramid* schemes that bring wealth to a few are also fraud.

4. Stealing is shameful.

Proverbs 19:26 (NIV) [26] *He who robs his father and drives out his mother is a son who brings shame and disgrace.*

An addict who steals from family members so he/she can continue in their sinful habit is shameful and only brings disgrace upon the family. Robbing from anyone, no matter how small the item or amount, is shameful. The taking of company property without asking is shameful. Dishonest behavior becomes a slippery slope that leads to more corruption. We need to be honest in all of our dealings and fair with everyone. We are easily disgusted with the man who steals someone's hard-earned savings; but we need to be just as upset with small items that are stolen from others. The pen, notepad, etc…

5. Stealing is not loving my brother

Romans 13:10 (NIV) [10] Love does no harm to its neighbor. Therefore love is the fulfillment of the law.

If you owned a company that provided pens for your employees, would you be upset if you had to buy more and more pens because people were taking them home for personal use? It would be one thing if you purchased the pens and encouraged your employees to take them home and pass them out. But it would be altogether different, if you did not authorize the pens for personal use. It would be stealing. The pens are your property. The employees are to respect your property and your wishes.

We justify sin in our minds by thinking one pen isn't going to matter. One pen probably won't make the business go broke, but it is still a sin that has a ripple effect in society.

Stealing is stealing; no matter how small the item. It is not loving your brother. It is considering yourself better than the person you are stealing from. We are not to do anything that harms our brother; not even the taking of one pen.

As believers, we are to set the highest standards of holiness. We are to be the examples of righteousness in society. Romans 2:21 (NIV) [21] *You, then, who teach others, do you not teach yourself? You who preach against stealing, do you steal?*

The context and the question is probing for us down to the smallest detail. Do you preach against stealing big things; but steal small things for your own benefit? Do you use yesterday's McDonald's cup or gas station cup to steal a refill for today? All forms of stealing are immoral. No stealing is acceptable.

SIN GROWS AND AFFECTS MORE

When we turn away from God's restraints, we open doors for great evil. Satan loves to trick us and get us to justify sin. In doing this, sin's power grows and does great harm to others. Has it benefitted our society to stop teaching the Ten Commandments in our public educational system? Do we have politicians with integrity and honest scales? Do those on Wall Street consider others before themselves?

Romans 6:16 (NIV) [16] Don't you know that when you offer yourselves to someone to obey him as slaves, you are slaves to the one whom you obey—whether you are slaves to sin, which leads to death, or to obedience, which leads to righteousness?

Our nation is where it is today because we have not taken the time to teach our children the Ten Commandments. They have not been shown how to follow them carefully. Each time we justify stealing, we only become more enslaved by it.

STEALING MAKES THE TEACHINGS ABOUT GOD UNATTRACTIVE

We can make the teaching of God attractive by protecting each other's property and respecting what they own. When we are encouraged to cut a corner for our own benefit, we need to say no. We need to teach others to love their neighbors as themselves. Proverbs 1:10-19 (NIV) [10] My son, if sinners entice you, do not give in to them. [11] If they say, "Come along with us; let's lie in wait for someone's blood, let's waylay some harmless soul; [12] let's swallow them alive, like the grave, and whole, like those who go down to the pit; [13] we will get all sorts of valuable things and fill our houses with plunder; [14] throw in your lot with us, and we will share a common purse"– [15] my son, do not go along with them, do not set foot on their paths; [16] for their feet rush into sin, they are swift to shed blood. [17] How useless to spread a net in full view of all the birds! [18] These men lie in wait for their own blood; they waylay only themselves! [19] Such is the end of all who go after ill-gotten gain; it takes away the lives of those who get it.

Titus 2:9-10 (NIV) [9] Teach slaves to be subject to their masters in everything, to try to please them, not to talk back to them, [10] and not to steal from them, but to show that they can be **fully trusted**, so that in every way they will make the teaching about God our Savior attractive.

When we obey the teachings of Christ and carefully follow the Ten Commandments, we make the teachings of Christ attractive. We show the world how to live respectfully toward God and others.

If you had a valuable possession and needed to trust someone with it while you went away, who would you choose? Would you choose a person who cut corners for their own benefit or someone with high integrity? Would you choose a co-worker who was stealing from the boss or the employee who worked hard and could be **fully trusted**? Christians should shine like stars in their communities as the most trustworthy individuals.

Philippians 2:12-15 (NIV) [12] Therefore, my dear friends, as you have always obeyed—not only in my presence, but now much more in my absence—continue to work out your salvation with fear and trembling, [13] for it is God who works in you to will and to act according to his good purpose. [14] Do everything without complaining or arguing, [15] so that you may become blameless and pure, children of God without fault in a crooked and depraved generation, in which you shine like stars in the universe.

We live in a crooked and depraved society where people steal from one another. This behavior is sometimes justified by the fact that so many are doing it. But we are not to look at the behavior of those around us for our guidance. We are to work out our salvation with fear and trembling; knowing that one day we will stand before Christ and be judged based upon His commands. All forms of stealing, no matter how accepted they may become in society, will be judged as criminal acts. Remember what Paul said in Romans, Chapter 2, *"You who preach against stealing, do you steal?"* Paul is referring to even the smallest violation and the high integrity that we are to uphold as Christians. We are to be self-governed individuals. We are to maintain high standards in every institution; especially the institution of civil government.

Our laws discourage people from stealing, but laws alone are not enough. We must come alongside people and teach them how to follow Christ. The sooner we teach the commands of God, especially to our younger generations, the more trustworthy our nation will become. Those who have been stealing, even the small things, must learn how to love their neighbors and serve them. *Ephesians 4:28 (NIV) 28 He who has been stealing must steal no longer, but must work, doing something useful with his own hands, that he may have something to share with those in need.*

We can become the nation who slept with unlocked doors and unlocked cars once again, if we return to following God's commands.

THE GREATEST THIEF

Satan is a master thief. One of his greatest joys is stealing our freedoms and placing us into the bonds of slavery. *John 10:10 (NIV) 10 The thief comes only to steal and kill and destroy; I have come that they may have life, and have it to the full.* Ever since the Garden of Eden, he has been twisting God's laws and encouraging people to disobey them.

Adam and Eve lived in a beautiful place with no sin. They were free to own everything. They had dominion over the land and the animals. It was only when they listened to Satan, and ate the apple, that they lost many of their freedoms. We still feel the affects of their sin today; which is why we must cling to Christ and His commands. Christ is the only way for us to avoid further slavery.

Satan's goal is for an evil tyrant rule the world. In the last days, the antichrist will appear. It will be an oppressive land, especially for Christians. We can't avoid this tyrant's rule. He has been written about in the Scriptures and his reign will come to pass. But what if Christ's return is not for many years to come? Are there things we can do to avoid an increasingly oppressive society today? Yes! We can obey the Ten Commandments and the teachings of Christ. God desires to give us property and liberty, but we must obey His commands.

Have you ever noticed what the Sermon on the Mount says about dominion? *Matthew 6:9-13 (NIV)* *[9] "This, then, is how you should pray: "'Our Father in heaven, hallowed be your name, [10]* **your kingdom come, your will be done on earth** *as it is in heaven. [11] Give us today our daily bread. [12] Forgive us our debts, as we also have forgiven our debtors. [13] And lead us not into temptation, but deliver us from the evil one.'*

Christ has dominion over all things. He is the One who owns it all. We are just His servants. If we want God's will to be done on the earth, then we must submit to following Him and the example He set for us. We are to surrender our lives to His rule. Should our government be saying, *"God's will be done on earth as it is in heaven?"* Yes, most definitely. But instead they promote separation of church and state. Government no longer wants to know God's will in civil matters. As a result, we are now experiencing the consequences of fewer and fewer freedoms.
We have the choice to obey or not to obey, but remember that curses follow disobedience. God has dominion over all and His kingdom will reign forever. *Daniel 4:3 (NIV)* *³ How great are his signs, how mighty his wonders!* **His kingdom is an eternal kingdom; his dominion endures from generation to generation.** How did the Israelites become free from their tyrannical rule? Did they overpower the stronger Egyptians? No. God brought them out of the land of slavery. He gave them their freedom when they obeyed His laws. God's rule will keep a nation free, but the freedom is dependent upon obedience to His commands.

We are in a war with Satan. He wants to steal what God wants us to have. *Ephesians 6:10-12 (NIV)*
¹⁰ Finally, be strong in the Lord and in his mighty power.
¹¹ Put on the full armor of God so that you can take your stand against the devil's schemes. ¹² For our struggle is not agai nst flesh and blood, but against the rulers, against the authorities, against the powers of this dark

world and against the spiritual forces of evil in the heavenly realms.

It is God's mighty power that keeps a nation free. It is God's un-protection that allows a nation to go into slavery. *Exodus 23:22 (NIV) 22 If you listen carefully to what he says and do all that I say, I will be an enemy to your enemies and will oppose those who oppose you. Exodus 23:27 (NIV) 27 "I will send my terror ahead of you and throw into confusion every nation you encounter. I will make all your enemies turn their backs and run.* If we want to keep our own property and live long in the land, then we must turn our lives over to the dominion of Christ. He will govern us if we submit to Him and His laws. Satan seeks to steal, kill and destroy. Satan's deception and lies get people to turn away from God and chase after the things of this world.

According to God's Word, we have a responsibility to govern, to rule, and to have dominion in the land. How are we to govern in a civil society? First, we must focus on Self-government by learning the teachings of Christ. Second, we must understand how the family is to govern themselves. Third, we must know how the church is to govern. And finally, we must recognize our responsibility to lead in the civil arena and follow the Ten Commandments. The American Constitution will only work if we govern ourselves based upon the Word of God. He is the One True God. He is the only one who can protect us, sustain us, and provide for us.

Reverend Mathias Burnet once said, *"Let not your children have reason to curse you for giving up those rights and prostrating those institutions which your fathers delivered to you."* In the formation of America, our founding fathers sought to establish a Biblical Christian nation, one based upon the Word of God. While the constitution is not perfect, it does lay a good groundwork for this nation to remain free. But we must have Christian leaders who are willing to step up and serve.

WHAT DID THE FOREFATHERS ESTABLISH?

As the nation of Israel grew, Jethro, Moses's father-in-law, gave Moses some godly wisdom. Jethro, while visiting Moses, saw all that God was doing. The Bible says in *Exodus 18:13-23 (NIV)* [13] *The next day Moses took his seat to serve as judge for the people, and they stood around him from morning till evening.* [14] *When his father-in-law saw all that Moses was doing for the people, he said, "What is this you are doing for the people? Why do you alone sit as judge, while all these people stand around you from morning till evening?"* [15] *Moses answered him, "Because the people come to me to seek God's will.* [16] *Whenever they have a dispute, it is brought to me, and I decide between the parties and inform them of God's decrees and laws."* [17] *Moses' father-in-law replied, "What you are doing is not good.* [18] *You and these people who come to you will only wear yourselves out. The work is too heavy for you; you cannot handle it alone.* [19] *Listen now to me and I will give you some advice, and may God be with you. You must be the people's representative before God and bring their disputes to him. [20] Teach them the decrees and laws, and show them the way to live and the duties they are to perform. [21] But select capable men from all the people—men who fear God, trustworthy men who hate dishonest gain—and appoint them as officials over thousands, hundreds, fifties and tens. [22] Have them serve as judges for the people at all times, but have them bring every difficult case to you; the simple cases they can decide themselves. That will make your load lighter, because they will share it with you. [23] If you do this and God so commands, you will be able to stand the strain, and all these people will go home satisfied."*

This is exactly what Moses did. It lightened his load and the people went home satisfied. This is the pattern our government is based upon. We have people to rule over us locally and nationally. We have a Supreme Court to rule in the hard cases. We have judges to rule in each town. We have God-given laws to govern our lives by. Everything is in place to rule the land in righteousness.

The problem is that we have neglected to raise our children to know God's laws. We have forgotten to train ourselves to govern in civil offices. Where are the capable men who fear God, are trustworthy, and hate dishonest gain? Many of the people currently in civil offices are trying to do the best they can. Their services and sacrifices for our nation are appreciated. But the key to our nation remaining free is having one source of law to govern our republic and seeking God for His providence. This is the groundwork that our founders established.

Christian men and women must be willing to serve as judges, mayors, aldermen, congressmen, and senators. We need people who know and fear the commands of God to rule in the land. We need parents to raise their children to rule in righteousness in the land. We cannot rule with wisdom, if we do not know God's prohibitions and laws.

What can we do? How can we save our nation from further decay?

1. Admit our sin

I Kings 8:46-51 (NIV) [46] *"When they sin against you—for there is no one who does not sin—and you become angry with them and give them over to the enemy, who takes them captive to his own land, far away or near;* [47] *and if they have a change of heart in the land where they are held captive, and repent and plead with you in the land of their conquerors and say, 'We have sinned, we have done wrong, we have acted wickedly';* [48] *and if they turn back to you with all their heart and soul in the land of their enemies who took them captive, and pray to you toward the land you gave their fathers, toward the city you have chosen and the temple I have built for your Name;* [49] *then from heaven, your dwelling place, hear their prayer and their plea, and uphold their cause.* [50] *And forgive your people, who have sinned against you; forgive all the offenses they have committed against you, and cause their conquerors to show them mercy; ⁵¹ for they are your people and your inheritance, whom you brought out of Egypt, out of that iron-smelting furnace.*

Our founders laid a good foundation for us. They encouraged us to live self-governed lives based upon the Word of God. They even endorsed the Bible to be distributed in America. These leaders pointed us to obey God and His Word.

2. Return to God's law

*Nehemiah 9:28-29 (NIV) ²⁸ "But as soon as they were at rest, they again did what was evil in your sight. Then you abandoned them to the hand of their enemies so that they ruled over them. And when they cried out to you again, you heard from heaven, and in your compassion you delivered them time after time. ²⁹ "**You warned them to return to your law**, but they became arrogant and disobeyed your commands. They sinned against your ordinances, by which a man will live if he obeys them. Stubbornly they turned their backs on you, became stiff-necked and refused to listen.*

There is a reason that the Ten Commandments are posted on so many buildings in the United States. It used to be the law that we agreed to obey and teach to our children. We must return to God's law and turn away from our stubborn hearts. This is what will heal our land. Our nation is in a mess because we have turned away from God. We must return to

God in our homes by having daily Bible readings, praying, and teaching the four Biblical institutions to our children. Families that have returned to the Lord need to help other families return to the Lord. Our command is to go and make disciples. We are to go and make other followers of Jesus who walk in His ways and know His laws.

I believe that the Ten Commandments should be taught in our homes and public schools. I believe that we should be praying to God in the White House, school house, church house, and in all of our houses.

Where is the superintendent who will bring prayer back to the local school? Where is the candidate who will run with the agenda of returning to the Ten Commandments and the teachings of Christ? George Washington, John Adams, Thomas Jefferson, and Abraham Lincoln are just a few of the many men who believed in such an agenda. Where are men like them now? Most men today are committed to things that do not produce eternal value or sustain the land of the free. We need to turn away from our comforts and lead our society the way God called us to.

3. Be fully committed to God

I Kings 8:56-61 (NIV) [56] *"Praise be to the LORD, who has given rest to his people Israel just as he promised. Not one word has failed of all the good promises he gave through his servant Moses.* [57] *May the LORD our God be with us as he was with our fathers; may he never leave us nor forsake us. ⁵⁸ May he turn our hearts to him, to walk in all his ways and to keep the commands, decrees and regulations he gave our fathers. ⁵⁹ And may these words of mine, which I have prayed before the LORD, be near to the LORD our God day and night, that he may uphold the cause of his servant and the cause of his people Israel according to each day's need, ⁶⁰ so that all the peoples of the earth may know that the LORD is God and that there is no other. ⁶¹ But your hearts must be fully committed to the LORD our God, to live by his decrees and obey his commands, as at this time."*

Are we fully committed to God? Will we do our part by teaching our children and raising them to be leaders in society? Will we speak up and tell our elected officials that we want prayer back in public places? Will we speak up and tell our elected officials that we want the Ten Commandments on our public buildings and taught in our public schools? Will we come alongside another and disciple them into being a follower of Christ? Will we understand that God created us to rule in the land and pray about leading in the civil arena?

It would be useless to begin such a movement if we are not individually committed to God. If we say that we want a return to the Ten Commandments, but we are not willing to obey the Sabbath command, the command not to steal, or any other command, then our efforts will be useless. If we say that we want to return to the Bible as our only source for law, but we are unwilling to read, study, and teach it to others; then our efforts will be useless. We must be fully committed to the Lord our God, live by His decrees, and obey his commands if we want to begin a second Great Awakening in this land.

Will we return to being *one nation under God?* Or will we continue to turn away from Him and suffer the consequences?

WORKSHEET FOR CIVIL GOVERNMENT
LIFE TRUTH # 8
YOU SHALL NOT STEAL

Question: What does it mean to steal?
Answer: Stealing is a violation of a person's God given right to rule their own property.

Exodus 20:15 (NIV) [15] *"You shall not steal."*

> Write out the Life Truth, question, and answer on one side of an index card and the verse on the other side. Keep it in your Bible for the week. Work on it every day individually and as a family. Have it memorized by next week.

Read Lev. 6:1-7. According to verse 4 what are we to do if we have stolen something?

Some types of stealing:
Embezzlement is the misuse or misappropriation of something that has been entrusted to you. (Lev. 6:2) How have people embezzled from others?

Read Isaiah 61:8. **Robbery** is when a person takes what belongs to another; many times with a weapon. How have people robbed from others?

Read Ezekiel 22:29; Luke 3:12-14. **Extortion** is when a person misuses their authority and takes from another or forces them to do something; most of the time without a weapon. (police officer, government, leader) How have people used extortion to steal from others?

Read Exodus 21:16; Deuteronomy 24:7; **Kidnapping** is taking someone by force to make them a slave or to hold for ransom. What was the punishment in the Old Testament for kidnapping?

Read Exodus 22:5. **Negligence** is when we are responsible for our property and neglectfully we have allowed our property to take (steal) from another. How have people been neglectful and stolen from others?

Read Psalm 37:21; Deuteronomy 22:1-4. **Not returning borrowed or found items.** How have people stolen in this way?

Read Deuteronomy 24:6. **Hurting someone's livelihood;** God is very concerned about people being free – owning their own property, and being productive in society. How do people hurt other's livelihood? (example: employees who don't work at work)

(T or F) Taking something small from a wealthy company is not stealing, but taking something big from a small company is.

Read Ephesians 4:28. How are thieves to be rehabilitated?

Based on this LIFE TRUTH, how can you help protect other people's property? How can you help others understand more about the serious consequences of stealing?

CIVIL GOVERNMENT
LIFE TRUTH # 9
YOU SHALL NOT LIE

The phrase *"false testimony against your neighbor"* is referring to perjury; or the breaking of an oath to tell the truth. In our nation, witnesses must take an oath of honesty. Witnesses place their right hand in the air and their left hand upon a Bible as they answer the following oath: "Do you swear to tell the truth, the whole truth, and nothing but the truth, so help you God?" When presidents are sworn in, they take the presidential oath. It is a constitutional law for the elected candidate to take this oath before their term begins. (Article 2, Section 1) The presidential oath of office says, "*I do solemnly swear (or affirm) that I will faithfully execute the Office of President of the United States, and will to the best of my ability, preserve, protect and defend the Constitution of the United States.*" This oath marks the end of one presidential term and the beginning of another.

All but two of our presidents have placed their hands upon a Bible and taken this oath. Many presidents have taken the oath with their Bibles opened to a specific verse. You can go to www.inaugural.senate.gov/swearing-in/bibles to see the Bibles and verses that presidential candidates have selected in the past. From the very first inauguration, when George Washington placed his hand upon the Bible and recited the oath, the inaugural ceremony has been an important symbol in our government's history.

Theodore Roosevelt was one of the men who did not place his hand upon a Bible to take the presidential oath. This was most likely due to the fact that he was sworn in when William McKinley, the current president, was on his death bed (William McKinley was assassinated when Theodore Roosevelt was Vice President).

The other candidate who did not place his hand upon the Bible was John Quincy Adams. Adams was sworn in as our sixth president on March 4, 1825. He placed his hand on the Book of Law instead of the Bible. Some have interpreted Quincy's choice as an effort to encourage separation of church and state. However, in his inaugural address (www.inaugural.senate.gov/swearing-in/event/john-quincy-adams-1825), Adams clearly expressed his religious convictions and was in no way encouraging such a separation. He said in his address, *"I appear, my fellow-citizens, in your presence and in that of Heaven to bind myself by the solemnities of* **religious obligation** *to the faithful performance of the duties allotted to me in the station to which I have been called."* He ends his address with these words, *"I shall look for whatever success may attend my public service; and knowing that* **"except the Lord keep the city the watchman waketh but in vain,"** *with fervent supplications for His favor, to His overruling providence I commit with humble*

183

but fearless confidence my own fate and the future destinies of my country."

There was such an outcry in the nation after John Quincy Adams placed his hand on a book other than the Bible, that the Bible was quickly reinstituted into the ceremony. Our founders understood their religious obligation. They knew the source for law and freedom was the Word of God and they placed themselves under the authority of God's Word.

In the ninth commandment, we see the prohibition against lying stated in legal form. The Ten Commandments were given to the nation of Israel as a legal system for the nation to live by. This legal system is the same one our founders chose to base our nation upon. They understood that we have a religious obligation to abide by the laws of God and to walk in His ways. John Quincy Adams closed his inaugural address with, "*and knowing that except the Lord keep the city the watchman waketh but in vain,*" Adams was quoting a part of the passage in *Psalm 127:1 (NIV) Unless the LORD builds the house, its builders labor in vain. Unless the LORD watches over the city, the watchmen stand guard in vain.* He went on to say, "*with fervent supplications for His favor, to His overruling providence I commit with humble but fearless confidence my own fate and the future destinies of my country.*" *Supplications* mean prayers. He is telling us that he is going to pray fervently for God's favor and His overruling providence upon our land. This is religion in office.

Our nation has been blessed, and will only continue to be blessed, as we submit to Christ's authority in our lives. This is our religious obligation. Christianity is the rock on which this nation was built. It is the only rock that is able to sustain us.

Our republic is based upon God's law. Even though many of our laws originated from Scripture, they do not demand that we be Christians. The issue of where our source of law comes from still lies in the hands of the people. The Constitution is similar to the Bible in that it does not force anyone to be a Christian.

We are a nation that is made up of citizens who get to choose their leaders. We are a free people. Abraham Lincoln said, *"That this nation, under God, shall have a new birth of freedom – and that government of the people, by the people, for the people, shall not perish from the earth."* (End of the Gettysburg address November 19, 1863). Lincoln also said that people are the rightful masters of both Congress and the courts. They are not to overthrow the Constitution but instead overthrow the men who pervert the Constitution.

Our republic, as with any government, needed a source of law. The founders of our nation decided Christianity and God's Word would be the basis for all law and the foundation for all truth. The early leaders of our nation were voted in, by the people,

and were chosen because of their Biblical qualifications, "men who fear God, trustworthy men who hate dishonest gain." (Exodus 18:21)
The following quotes were made by godly men who helped to establish this great nation:

Thomas Jefferson - "When the people fear the government there is tyranny, when the government fears the people there is liberty."

John Jay, our first Supreme Court Justice said, "Providence has given to our people the choice of their rulers, and it is the duty, as well as the privilege and interest, of our **Christian nation** to select and prefer **Christians** for their rulers."

Noah Webster, considered the Father of Education said, "In my view, the **Christian religion** is the more important and one of the first things in which all children, under a free government ought to be instructed."
In June, 1775, President John Adams said, "We have appointed a Continental fast. Millions will be upon their knees at once before their great Creator, imploring his forgiveness and blessing."

In October, 1789, **George Washington** said, "It is the duty of all nations to acknowledge the providence of Almighty God, **to obey His will**, to be grateful for His benefits, and humbly to implore His protection and favor."

In 1803, at the National Day of Prayer Proclamation, President **Abraham Lincoln** said, "Whereas the

Senate of the United States, devoutly recognizing the supreme authority and just government of Almighty God in all the affairs of men and of nations, has by a resolution requested the President to designate and set apart a day for national prayer and humiliation."

William J. Federer wrote a book entitled <u>PRAYERS and PRESIDENTS</u> - Inspiring Faith from Leaders of the Past. This book is a vast collection of prayers by former civil leaders. It emphasizes the religious obligation needed in this country in order to be blessed. In the introduction of his book, Federer speaks about James Madison. **James Madison** is considered the *"Chief Architect of the Constitution."* He is also the man who introduced the first amendment; an amendment which is now the discussion of much hostile debate in our nation. Amendment I says, *"Congress shall make no law respecting an establishment of religion, or prohibiting the free exercise thereof; or abridging the freedom of speech, or of the press; or the right of the people peaceably to assemble, and to petition the Government for a redress of grievances."*

Our founders did not want to be bound by the Church of England or any other <u>established</u> religion that might come along. They longed to be a free people, guided only by the Word of God. They established a nation *"under God, with liberty and justice for all."* They believed that people should have the freedom to speak from their hearts and share their beliefs with others.

James Madison and the other founders succeeded. On July 9, 1812, President James Madison proclaimed a Day of Prayer, stating, *"I do therefore recommend...rendering the Sovereign of the Universe...public homage...acknowledging the transgressions which might justly provoke His divine displeasure...seeking His merciful forgiveness...and with a reverence for the unerring precept of our holy religion, to do to others as they would require that others should do to them."* This was issued during the War of 1812. President Madison asked the people to cry out to God for the forgiveness of their sins and to have reverence for the holy religion of Christianity. This is what he believed. This is what he called the people to do.

On July 23, 1813, Madison issued another Day of Prayer. He referred to *"religion, that gift of Heaven for the good of man."* Madison believed that if they carefully obeyed the laws of God and sought God's guidance for provisions and protection, that the Lord would hear their prayers and bless their land. The people of this nation responded and prayed, sought God's forgiveness, and obeyed the commands of God.

When the British marched on Washington, D.C., citizens evacuated, along with the President and Dolly Madison. The British burned the White House, Capitol, and other public buildings on August 25, 1814. Suddenly dark clouds rolled in and a tornado touched down. It sent debris flying, blowing off roofs, and knocking chimneys down on British troops. Two cannons were lifted off the ground and dropped yards away. A British historian wrote: *"More British soldiers were killed by this stroke of nature than from all the firearms the American troops had mustered. British forces then fled and rains extinguished the fires."*

Our founders believed the passage in *Deuteronomy 28:6-7 (NIV) ⁶ You will be blessed when you come in and blessed when you go out. ⁷ The LORD will grant that the enemies who rise up against you will be defeated before you. They will come at you from one direction but flee from you in seven.* They believed in the One True God. They knew that if they obeyed Him, He would bless them. They prayed in public buildings. They prayed in private buildings. They talked about God and His Word. They wrote about God in their manuscripts. They were men of valor, unafraid of the enemies around them. They knew that the Lord was on their side.

The first amendment ensures that no denomination can come into power and take over. No one group can ever dictate how to baptize, how to take the Lord's Supper, or how to give tithes and offerings. Some read the first amendment and believe it means that the government should stay out of religion all together. But the amendment actually says that the government should never prohibit the free exercise of religion. So when the government tells us that we cannot pray in a public place, they are breaking the first amendment. They are prohibiting the free exercise of a person's religion; exactly what the founders did not want. The founders wanted people to pray to God publicly and privately, asking Him to forgive them and bless them. God blessed America because of their faith and their Christian beliefs.

God will no longer fight for us or protect us if we turn away from Him. We will experience the curses that fall upon nations that turn their backs on God. Curses that include debt, violence, depression, disease, natural disasters, international conflicts, and harsh leaders that rule and drive us into slavery.

Which document holds greater authority: The United States Constitution or the Holy Word of God? Which document must be heeded with all our might and studied to understand its truth? The Bible is what must govern us. This was our first self-government life truth. Scripture alone is what governs us. **If the constitution disagrees with Scripture in any way we should change the constitution and not the Scripture!**

Some "conservatives" in our generation interpret the first amendment to mean that we should defend all of the religions that man may have. This is not true. The source of our law must be the Bible. Throughout history, there have been cases that have gone against a person's religious beliefs. Do you remember the case against Benjamin, the Jewish man who sold a pair of gloves on the Sabbath? Our judicial system ruled in favor of God's Word and not his religious beliefs.

Do you remember the case of Davis, the polygamist who stated that he was living according to his religious beliefs? Our nation ruled against him based upon Christian values found in the Word of God.

When we choose to go against the laws of God, we bring consequences upon ourselves. This is exactly where we are today. Are we a blessed nation or a cursed nation?

It is time for Christians to repent. We need to call upon God for his mercy and grace to heal our land once again. When we pray the Lord's Prayer, *"your kingdom come, your will be done, on earth as it is in heaven,"* do we understand the importance of this oath? God's ways should be the guidelines for our laws. If a person's religious beliefs harm somebody, or harm society, we need to rule in favor of God's will being done upon this earth. When we recite the Lord's Prayer, we take an oath in His name to do all that we can to bring His kingdom and His will to this earth. This is our responsibility to the Lord. *Matthew 28:19-20 (NIV) [19] Therefore go and make disciples of all nations, baptizing them in the name of the Father and of the Son and of the Holy Spirit, [20] and teaching them to obey everything I have commanded you. And surely I am with you always, to the very end of the age."*

We are to *teach* people the truth in God's Word. We are to *show* people how He expects us to live. This nation has real consequences for perjury. We understand the seriousness of this sin from the

Word of God. Our greatest fear about lying should be that one day we will stand before God and be judged for all our lies. *Revelation 21:8 (NIV) [8] But the cowardly, the unbelieving, the vile, the murderers, the sexually immoral, those who practice magic arts, the idolaters and **all liars**—their place will be in the fiery lake of burning sulfur. This is the second death."*

The ninth commandment needs to be taught. The consequences of being a liar need to be understood by all. No one wants a nation of liars and deceivers. No one wants to be lied to. Many times people lie to benefit themselves. They may get away with lies on this earth, but they are destroying society in the process. The child, who tells his parents that he has no homework, just so that he can go outside to play, should be warned of the serious consequences of this sin.

Lying is a grave offense toward God. We should be teaching our children that bearing false testimony is a crime. The fear of the Lord is the beginning of wisdom. God wants us to be people of our word. He wants us to always speak the truth.

Oaths

Court rooms today call witnesses to take an oath for honesty, but some leave off the phrase "*so help me God.*" The oath goes something like this, "*You do affirm that all the testimony you are about to give in the case now before the court will be the truth, the whole truth, and nothing but the truth; this you do affirm under the pains and penalties of perjury."*

Our fear has been transferred from a fear of God to a fear of the state. This is a problem in our generation. The state or the government is becoming the god that we fear; the god that we look to for help. We need to be looking to the Almighty God and asking Him to bless and provide for us as we submit to His will upon this earth. Our main focus should be to govern ourselves based upon His words.

In the court of law, one witness should not be enough to convict a person of a capital offense. The Bible addresses cases where a false witness may come forward and lie about another. A person may have hatred in their heart toward another and lie to get the person punished. The Bible says in Deuteronomy 19:15-21 (NIV) [15] *One witness is not enough to convict a man accused of any crime or offense he may have committed. A matter must be established by the testimony of two or three witnesses.* [16] *If a malicious witness takes the stand to accuse a man of a crime,* [17] *the two men involved in the dispute must stand in the presence of the LORD before the priests and the judges who are in office at the time.* [18] *The judges must make a thorough investigation, and if the witness proves to be a liar, giving false testimony against his brother,* [19] *then do to him as he intended to do to his brother. You must purge the evil from among you.* [20] *The rest of the people will hear of this and be afraid, and never again will such an evil thing be done among you.* [21] *Show no pity: life for* life, eye for eye, tooth for tooth, hand for hand, foot for foot.

God addressed this issue. Fairness should be administered in a righteous court. If only one witness comes forward, the case should be dismissed. If the person accusing is found guilty of bearing false testimony against their neighbor, then the court should administer the same punishment on the liar as they would have administered to the accused. The judgments must be fair.

Jesus addressed the issue of taking oaths. He sought to straighten out the offenses that the Pharisee's brought to the command. The Bible tells us to take our oaths only in the Lord's name. *Deuteronomy 6:13-14 (NIV)* [13] *Fear the LORD your God, serve him only and take your oaths in his name.* [14] *Do not follow other gods, the gods of the peoples around you;*

This is why when we come into a courtroom to be a witness we should say, "so help me God."

Jesus says in *Matthew 5:33-37 (NIV)* [33] *"Again, you have heard that it was said to the people long ago, 'Do not break your oath, but keep the oaths you have made to the Lord.'* [34] *But I tell you, Do not swear at all: either by heaven, for it is God's throne;* [35] *or by the earth, for it is his footstool; or by Jerusalem, for it is the city of the Great King.* [36] *And do not swear by your head, for you cannot make even one hair white or black.* [37] *Simply let your*

'Yes' be 'Yes,' and your 'No,' 'No'; anything beyond this comes from the evil one.

Jesus is not saying that we should never take an oath. Jesus is saying that we should only take an oath in His name. Psalm 63:11 (NIV) [11] But the king will rejoice in God; all who swear by God's name will praise him, while the mouths of liars will be silenced. He is also raising the level of all of our words to that of taking oaths. Everything we say whether it be a yes or a no is like taking an oath in the Lord's name.

Deuteronomy 23:21-23 (NIV) [21] If you make a vow to the LORD your God, do not be slow to pay it, for the LORD your God will certainly demand it of you and you will be guilty of sin. [22] But if you refrain from making a vow, you will not be guilty. [23] Whatever your lips utter you must be sure to do, because you made your vow freely to the LORD your God with your own mouth.

Jesus addressed the hypocritical laws that the Pharisee's were teaching to the people. The Pharisee's were adding their own rules to God's laws. They said that an oath could be sworn by heaven, the earth, or by Jerusalem without penalty. Jesus revealed how wrong their thinking was. He said, "Do not swear at all: either by heaven, for it is God's throne; [35] or by the earth, for it is his footstool; or by Jerusalem, for it is the city of the Great King."

God owns it all. He will judge us all on everything we have said, thought, and done.

Jesus used legal terms about our words in *Matthew 12:36-37 (NIV) ³⁶ But I tell you that men will have to give account on the day of judgment for every careless word they have spoken. ³⁷ For by your words you will be acquitted, and by your words you will be condemned."* We will all stand before God one day and be judged. We will give an account for what we have said. Our words will either convict us or acquit us. Our *yes* and our *no* should be as serious as if it was an oath to the Lord. We need to humble ourselves before an Almighty God and seek His forgiveness and mercy. We should be dependable, honest, and hardworking people that live to give God all the glory.

We need to make sure that we follow through on our word. When we fail, we need to ask those that we have disappointed to forgive us. We need to be more careful as to what we commit ourselves to do. When we tell our children that we will take them somewhere or that we will be home at a certain time, we must follow through or ask them for forgiveness. This must be done in all of our relationships. We are to be people of our word. Peter tells us that we should only speak words that God himself would speak. *I Peter 4:11 (NIV) ¹¹ If anyone speaks, he should do it as one speaking the very words of God.*

A nation that accepts lies crumbles because no one can be trusted. A righteous legal system is based upon truth and justice. Justice is distorted when lies are believed. The very foundation of liberty depends upon truth, justice, and mercy for those that are repentant. When lawyers distort words and their meanings to win cases, their positions of authority have been compromised. Winning is not the ultimate goal.

Where does our truth come from? Does it come from man? *Mark 7:21-23 (NIV) ²¹ For from within, out of men's hearts, come evil thoughts, sexual immorality, theft, murder, adultery, ²² greed, malice, deceit, lewdness, envy, slander, arrogance and folly. ²³ All these evils come from inside and make a man 'unclean.'"*

If a professor told you that at the end of the semester you would be given a test based upon a specific book, what should you do? Most would agree that in order to pass the test you should study the assigned textbook. What would happen on the day of the test if you studied the wrong book or didn't study at all? You would most likely fail miserably.

God has given us the Bible as our textbook. It has all the answers to life in it. If we do not study God's textbook, we will fail miserably at life. A nation of the people, by the people, and for the people, will crumble when we don't know the answers to God's questions of life.

Truth needs to be our ultimate pursuit. Jesus is the way, **the truth**, and the life. *John 14:6 (NIV) ⁶ Jesus* answered, "I am the way and the truth and the life. No one comes to the Father except through me.

The law was formed to keep us truthful. There are consequences to lies; consequences on the earth and consequences on the Day of Judgment. *I Timothy 1:8-11 (NIV)* *8 We know that the law is good if one uses it properly. 9 We also know that law is made not for the righteous but for lawbreakers and rebels, the ungodly and sinful, the unholy and irreligious; for those who kill their fathers or mothers, for murderers, 10 for adulterers and perverts, for slave traders and **liars and perjurers**—and for whatever else is contrary to the **sound doctrine** 11 that conforms to the glorious gospel of the blessed God, which he entrusted to me.*

Righteous laws are based upon "sound doctrine." It is our religious obligation to uphold sound Christian doctrine and protect the free exercise of religion. But we cannot uphold what we do not understand or know. The law not to murder comes from religion. The laws not to steal, lie, covet, or commit adultery all come from religion. The Christian religion is the foundation of righteous laws. **To remove religion from our civil responsibilities is to remove righteousness from our government.**

Satan is a liar. He has been lying from the very beginning of creation. God said in *Genesis 2:16-17 (NIV) 16 And the LORD God commanded the man, "You are free to eat from any tree in the garden; 17 but you* must not eat from the tree of the knowledge of good and evil, for when you eat of it **you will surely die**." Satan appeared in Genesis 3:4 (NIV) [4] "**You will not surely die,**" the serpent said to the woman.

Jesus spoke plainly about those who do not believe that He is God. John 8:42-47 (NIV) [42] Jesus said to them, "If God were your Father, you would love me, for I came from God and now am here. I have not come on my own; but he sent me. [43] Why is my language not clear to you? Because you are unable to hear what I say. [44] You belong to your father, the devil, and you want to carry out your father's desire. **He was a murderer from the beginning, not holding to the truth, for there is no truth in him. When he lies, he speaks his native language, for he is a liar and the father of lies.** [45] Yet because I tell the truth, you do not believe me! [46] Can any of you prove me guilty of sin? If I am telling the truth, why don't you believe me? [47] He who belongs to God hears what God says. The reason you do not hear is that you do not belong to God."

Those that desire to get God out of civil government do not understand that God established the governing authorities. Romans 13:1 (NIV) [1] Everyone must submit himself to the governing authorities, for there is no authority except that which God has established. The authorities that exist have been established by God. God places people in governing positions. They should thank him for the responsibility and the dominion that He has given them. They must also understand that there will be a higher judgment upon them due to their positions of authority.

Satan is encouraging separation of church and state by twisting the words of our first amendment. He is causing people to be blind regarding the historical facts of our nation's history. He misrepresented a letter that Thomas Jefferson wrote to the Danbury Baptist that ensured them that the government was not going to have an established religion ruling over them. Satan is very good at twisting the truth and causing people to believe His lies.

As long as God allows Satan to roam, we will have to defend the truth and stand up against his lies. The more we know of God's Word, the better we will be able to defend against the lies of Satan. We need to be a people of the Word of God. We need to repent and return to a love of God's Word. As long as we live in this republic, leaders will rise up from among our own people. We need men and women who fear God, are trustworthy, and hate dishonest gain.

Our history is not infallible. Many have made mistakes that have gone before us. Their mistakes are not the authority in how we should move forward. Our source of law remains the Holy Bible and its wisdom to guide us through our lives. We must remain one nation under God. We need to test the facts of both our history and our laws to make sure they match the Word of God.

If we do not know the truth, then how will we recognize a lie? American people, even in the church, are not committed to knowing Christian principles. We are not studying God's Word and therefore, we are guilty of bearing a false witness against our neighbors. If my neighbor believes that the sky is green and the grass is blue, and I do not tell them the truth, I am guilty. My silence bears a false witness of acceptance to his belief. Speak up for the truth. Do it in love, but speak up. Study the Scriptures! Be able to defend the truth! Proclaim where the source of truth lies.

Proverbs 3:5-8 (NIV) [5] Trust in the LORD with all your heart and lean not on your own understanding; [6] in all your ways acknowledge him, and he will make your paths straight. [7] Do not be wise in your own eyes; fear the LORD and shun evil. [8] This will bring health to your body and nourishment to your bones.

Psalm 119:105-106 (NIV) [105] Your word is a lamp to my feet and a light for my path. [106] I have taken an oath and confirmed it, that I will follow your righteous laws.

*John 8:31-32 (NIV) [31] To the Jews who had believed him, Jesus said, "**If you hold to my teaching**, you are really my disciples. [32] **Then you will know the truth, and the truth will set you free.**"*

George Washington said, "every officer and man should live, and act, as becomes a Christian Soldier defending the dearest rights and liberties of his country." George

Washington was known as a man of prayer. In the capital building in Washington D.C. there is a stained glass picture of President Washington kneeling in prayer with Psalm 16:1 written around him. *Psalm 16:1 (1599 Geneva Bible) [1] Preserve me, O GOD: for in thee do I trust".*

George Washington was not a shy man. He spoke up for the truth. He went around telling the troops not to cuss or play games of vice. He told them to attend Sunday services and to act like Christians. He believed in God's Word. He believed that Americans would be blessed **if they** obeyed God. He also said in his presidential proclamation for a day of prayer and thanksgiving on November 26, 1789. "*Whereas it is the duty of all nations to acknowledge the providence of Almighty God, to obey His will, to be grateful for His benefits, and humbly to implore His protection and favor.*"

We need people to stand up for Jesus and say, "Preserve me O God: for in thee do I trust." Where are men and women of valor? Where are the men and women who say that we should live and act *as becomes a Christian soldier?* Christian soldiers who do not use foul language, do not take the Lord's name in vain, who keep the Sabbath holy, and obey all Ten of the Commandments.

Throughout our history, we have made laws based upon religion, but never a law respecting an establishment of religion. The key word is establishment and not religion. No law has ever established the Catholic church as being the only church in the United States; nor will one ever establish any other denomination. Our early settlers left the established Church of England to worship God freely in a new land according to their own convictions.

The following are some of the religious laws that our government has made:

The Pledge of Allegiance was written in August, 1892 by the socialist minister, Francis Bellamy (1855-1931). It was originally published in *The Youth's Companion* on September 8, 1892. Bellamy had hoped for the pledge to be used by citizens in any country. In its original form it read: *"I pledge allegiance to my Flag and the Republic for which it stands, one nation, indivisible, with liberty and justice for all."*

In 1923, *"the Flag of the United States of America,"* was added.*"I pledge allegiance to the Flag of the United States of America and to the Republic for which it stands, one nation, indivisible, with liberty and justice for all."*

In 1954, in response to the Communist threat of the times, President Eisenhower encouraged Congress to add the words *"under God,"* creating the 31-word pledge we say today. Today it reads: **"I pledge allegiance to the flag of the United States of America, and to the republic for which it stands, one nation under God, indivisible, with liberty**

and justice for all." (Taken from http://www.ushistory.org/documents/pledge.htm)

In 1952, President Truman, along with the joint resolution of Congress, declared an annual National Day of Prayer.

In 1983, the Supreme Court affirmed the right of state legislatures to open their sessions with prayer (Marsh vs. Chambers).

In 1988, the law regarding the National Day of Prayer was amended and signed by President Reagan, permanently recognizing it on the first Thursday of every May. Last year, over 40,000 prayer meetings were held across our nation as a result of this law that was established by our government. The law reads: *The President shall issue each year a proclamation designating the first Thursday in May as a National Day of Prayer on which the people of the United States may turn to God in prayer and meditation at churches, in groups, and as individuals.*

These are definitely religious laws. All people should be able to pray in public and in private. It is our God-given right and our first amendment right as well.

Where are the people who will stand up for truth in our nation? Where are the men and women who will follow the guidelines established by our founders? Where are those who will say that we must obey

God rather than man and point people to the Word of God as our only source of law once again?

Lying is an intentional deception away from the truth. This includes being silent. What has God called Christians who know the truth to do? *Acts 1:8 (NIV) ⁸ But you will receive power when the Holy Spirit comes on you; and you will be my __witnesses__ in Jerusalem, and in all Judea and Samaria, and to the ends of the earth."*

When people around us believe lies, we should tell them the truth. We should speak up for God and His Word. **To be silent only makes them feel that we accept what they believe as the truth.** The Great Commission, in Matthew 28, tells us to teach them to obey all things that Christ taught. The Lord's Prayer is our oath to bring God's will upon the earth.

We have religious obligations with a free and blessed nation. Christians are to speak up and tell the truth according to God's Word. If a person believes that a marriage does not have to be between a man and a woman, we need to tell them exactly what the Bible says in Romans, Chapter 1. If we are told not to pray in Jesus name, we must break man's law and obey God's law. If we are told not to take our personal Bibles to school, we must break man's law and obey God's law. If we are forbidden to pray in school or to teach the Ten Commandments, we must break man's law and obey God's law. This is what Daniel did. This is what Shadrach, Meshach, and Abednego did. This is what the prophets and the apostles did. Which law holds greater weight with you? Man's law or God's law?

Where are the men and women who will lead us in this generation? If we want to be free from our debt; if we want to heal our families and marriages; if we want to lessen the violence in our nation; if we want to see truth prevail and distorted and twisted untruths silenced; then we must humble ourselves before Almighty God, confess our sins, and return to obedience. We must obey God's Ten Commandments.

WORKSHEET FOR CIVIL GOVERNMENT
LIFE TRUTH # 9
YOU SHALL NOT LIE

Question: What does it mean to lie?
Answer: Lying is an intentional deception away from the truth.

Exodus 20:16 (NIV) ¹⁶ *"You shall not give false testimony against your neighbor.*

> Write out the Life Truth, question, and answer on one side of an index card and the verse on the other side. Keep it in your Bible for the week. Work on it every day individually and as a family. Have it memorized by next week.

Read Proverbs 6:16-19; 19:5, 9; 21:28. What do these passages reveal to us about how God views a false witness?

Read Deuteronomy 17:6; 19:15 Why is it important not to convict a person with capital punishment on the basis of just one witness?

List a few reasons why people do not tell the truth.

Read Proverbs 11:11-13. A gossip is someone who goes about spreading harmful information about another. At times, the gossip sensationalizes the truth and or twists the truth. How is gossiping bearing a false testimony against our neighbor?

Why do you think people gossip?

How can gossip hurt others?

What can you do to guard against gossiping?

Read Ephesians 4:14-16. How could someone speak the truth without love?

Read Deuteronomy 6:13-14; 23:21-23. How does God feel about oaths that we take in His name?

(T or F) This is a lie: A parent asks their child if they have brushed their teeth. It is bedtime and the parent is questioning the child to see if they have brushed their teeth before going to bed. The child who does not want to get out of bed remains in bed and says, "Yes". The child justifies this in their mind by saying, "I did this morning."

Our current judiciary system plays word games to get around the truth. Lawyers do this a lot in our generation. Why is this dangerous to a society?

Explain this statement: Lying to others is hiding who you really are.

Read Revelation 21:6-8. What is the fate of all liars?

Based on this LIFE TRUTH, what can we do to guard ourselves against lying and gossiping? How can you help others understand more about the serious consequences of lying?

CIVIL GOVERNMENT
LIFE TRUTH # 10
YOU SHALL NOT COVET

The Hebrew word for *covet* translates to mean *"to desire"* in the tenth commandment. This commandment is not suggesting that every desire is sinful. It is speaking about ungoverned desires that threaten the rights of others and are very dangerous to society. It is God's plan for all people to govern their own property and control their covetous desires.

Our founders understood that God endowed every person with life, liberty, and the pursuit of happiness. The pursuit of happiness is a phrase that the founders used to describe a person's ability to own and govern their own property. The Fifth Amendment of the U.S. Constitution says, *"nor be deprived of life, liberty, or property, without due process of law; nor shall private property be taken for public use, without just compensation."*

Being free involves the ability to make choices and decisions about ourselves and our property. This includes our political freedoms. Government leaders have the responsibility to protect the rights of the righteous and bridle the covetous desires of others by punishing evil doers. If leaders abuse their powers, they enslave people by taking away their freedoms. We have seen the devastation of this in countries that have had tyrants who have ruled oppressively.

For a land to remain free, we need to understand what Noah Webster said in his article entitled, *Letters to a Young Gentleman Commencing His Education*, published in 1823. He said, *"In selecting men of office, let principle be your guide…It is alleged by men of loose principles, or defective views on the subject, that religion and morality are not necessary or important qualifications for political stations.* **But the Scriptures teach a different doctrine.** *They direct that rulers should be men who rule in the fear of God, able men, such as fear God, men of truth, hating covetousness."* (Exodus 18:21)

Today's generation believes that what goes on in a person's "private life" doesn't affect their ability to be a leader in society. This is nonsense! It matters greatly how a person conducts their "private life," as to how they will lead at the city gate. For example, if a man covets someone else's wife and selfishly has to have her, then he has disqualified himself as a man who is interested in protecting the rights of others. He has himself committed a crime against his neighbor. How can he protect the righteous and punish the evil doer if he himself is an evil doer?

Religion and morality are vital to our nation remaining free. The government should not control our healthcare, welfare, or any other area of life that affects our property. God desires for us to be a free people who govern our own possessions.

Biblically, the government is to enforce just laws, protect the righteous, and punish those who do not love their neighbors as themselves.

When a government takes over property rights and no longer thinks that the quality of a person's character is important for the men and women seeking office, we are headed for disaster. *You shall not covet* is foundational to a society that wishes to remain free.

Coveting is setting our hearts, or desires, upon earthly things instead of setting our hearts upon God's kingdom. America is a very covetous society. People are paid lots of money to design commercials that encourage viewers to covet. In fact, their main goal is to stir a desire within us to have their product. Some advertisers even go as far as using pornography to try to bring a sexual excitement to their product.

What drives a person to influence others to break the tenth commandment? Most often, it is their covetous desire for money. It takes them down a destructive path and blinds them to the very fact that they are causing other people to sin. Many times advertisers direct their covetous campaigns to young people in hopes of securing better product sales in the future. Perhaps advertisers should learn the tenth commandment before they begin the process of an advertising campaign. They should heed the Words of Christ in *Matthew 18:6-7 (NIV)* [6] *But if anyone causes one of these little ones who believe in me to sin, it would be better for him to have a large millstone hung around his neck and to be drowned in the depths of the sea. ⁷ "Woe to the world because of the things that cause people to sin! Such things must come, but woe to the man through whom they come!*

The more covetous a society, the more pain a nation endures. When people stop using self-restraint by allowing their earthly passions to be aroused, they begin to compromise their beliefs. They let down their morals and allow selfish desires to rule their decisions. People who want power will say anything to get votes. People who want wealth will do anything to achieve riches.

The tenth commandment specifically protects a person's God-given right to rule their own property. Exodus 20:17 (NIV) ¹⁷ *"You shall not covet your neighbor's house. You shall not covet your neighbor's wife, or his manservant or maidservant, his ox or donkey, or anything that belongs to your neighbor."* God is very specific in the command. We are not to desire anything that belongs to our neighbor. We are to protect the rights of each other and not become jealous or envious of what others have. The Bible describes a society governed by the Word of God in Romans 13:10 (NIV) ¹⁰ *Love does no harm to its neighbor. Therefore love is the fulfillment of the law.*

The prophet, Micah, gives a stern warning to those who abuse their positions of authority in a covetous way. *Micah 2:1-2 (NIV) ¹ Woe to those who plan iniquity, to those who plot evil on their beds! At morning's light they carry it out because it is in their power to do it. ² They covet fields and seize them, and houses, and take them. They defraud a man of his home, a fellowman of his inheritance.*

People often abuse God-given positions of authority. Horrible offenses have been committed against children as parents have abused their roles. Horrible offenses have been committed against spouses and families as mates have coveted the wife or husband of another. Horrible offenses have been committed against people as governments have confiscated their property and possessions in order to gain power and strength.

God warns us that we need to be very careful with our unbridled passions. Our focus must be on Him and His will for our lives. *Galatians 5:13-17 (NIV) ¹³ You, my brothers, were called to be free. But do not use your freedom to indulge the sinful nature; rather, serve one another in love. ¹⁴ The entire law is summed up in a single command: "Love your neighbor as yourself." ¹⁵ If you keep on biting and devouring each other, watch out or you will be destroyed by each other. ¹⁶ So I say, live by the Spirit, and you will not gratify the desires of the sinful nature. ¹⁷ For the sinful nature desires what is contrary to the Spirit, and the Spirit what is contrary to the sinful nature. They are in conflict with each other, so that you do not do what you want.*

The passage says, *"If you keep on biting and devouring each other, watch out or you will be destroyed by each other."* By coveting other people's property, we begin the process of destruction. Our hearts are not set on love, forgiveness, and mercy. Instead, they are set upon our wants. As a covetous society, we eventually begin to destroy one another. People in control of money steal from others. People in positions of authority abuse power. Everyone focuses on what they want instead of what Christ wants.

The only way to control our sinful passions is by asking Jesus to be the Lord of our lives. The gift of God's Holy Spirit then fills us with the self-control we need. Our focus changes from earthly passions to loving God and others. *Colossians 3:1-2 (NIV) [1] Since, then, you have been raised with Christ, set your hearts on things above, where Christ is seated at the right hand of God. [2] Set your minds on things above, not on earthly things.*

The Ten Commandments were given in God's perfect order. The last command to not covet causes us reflect on our own desires. This reflection takes us back to the greatest command; we are to love God first. How do we love God first? We show God our love first by setting our hearts upon heavenly things and by obeying His Ten Commandments.
The Ten Commandments are the laws we must obey to honor God. When we break any of the commandments, we commit a crime. Remember, a

crime is committing an act that is forbidden. God forbids us to covet when he says, *"You shall not covet."* Coveting is a crime even before any property is stolen. Many know that King David committed the crime of adultery with Bathsheba. But did you know that he committed the crime of coveting before the crime of adultery? 2 Samuel 11:2-4 (NIV) *[2] One evening David got up from his bed and walked around on the roof of the palace. From the roof he saw a woman bathing. The woman was very beautiful, [3] and David sent someone to find out about her. The man said, "Isn't this Bathsheba, the daughter of Eliam and the wife of Uriah the Hittite?" [4] Then David sent messengers to get her. She came to him, and he slept with her. (She had purified herself from her uncleanness.) Then she went back home.*

David commits adultery in verse four, but he commits the crime of coveting in verse three. In verse two, he sees a beautiful woman bathing. At that point, he should have set his heart on things above and turned away from the woman. In verse three, he sends someone to find out about her and is told that she is the property of another man. Even the person sent to find out about her poses a question to David, reminding him that she is another man's wife, *"Isn't this Bathsheba, the daughter of Eliam and <u>the wife of Uriah</u> the Hittite?"* David does not set his heart on things above. He covets and sets his heart on earthly things; specifically another man's wife. *"Do not covet your neighbor's wife,"* the commandment states. This is a crime and a sin. Jesus says that if you lust after a woman in your heart, then you are guilty of committing adultery.

Coveting is in the mind even before the specific act is committed. It is as much a crime as anything, including stealing, lying, or adultery. The bank robber commits the crime of coveting other people's money even before he commits the crime of stealing. The owner of a company who covets wealth and power over truth is guilty of coveting even before he commits the sin of lying. Coveting can be hidden from man, but not from God. It is a warning light for our hearts. It lets us know that we are in danger of harming another person. As God's children, we are not to covet anything that belongs to our neighbor or harm them in any way.

We must seek God's kingdom first; not the things of this earth. **A society that knows coveting is a sin can prevent the pain and harm that comes from meditating upon our wants. Meditating upon the things of God, loving Him, and loving others is to be our focus.**

James 1:13-15 (NIV) [13] When tempted, no one should say, "God is tempting me." For God cannot be tempted by evil, nor does he tempt anyone; [14] but each one is tempted when, by his own evil desire, he is dragged away and enticed. [15] Then, after desire has conceived, it gives birth to sin; and sin, when it is full-grown, gives birth to death. When we set our hearts on our selfish desires, we act in sinful ways. We need to deny ourselves, pick up our crosses, and follow the example of Christ.

Even King David who was called, *"a man after God's own heart,"* set his heart on earthly things and was overcome by his passions. Only in Christ, can we be free to walk by the Spirit and truly love our neighbors. Christ gives us the ability to love one another. It is through Him that we can have a free society and respect each other's property. His laws allow us to live long in the land and not devour one another.

God established the four Biblical institutions in order for nations to be free and to remain free. The word nation or nations is used over 600 times in the Bible. God has a plan for all nations. He desires that all nations be free and blessed, but it is dependent upon them submitting to His Lordship and obeying His word. The following passage in Psalms reveals that blessed nations are built by families who submit to the Lordship of Jesus.

Psalm 96:7-10 (NIV) [7] *Ascribe to the LORD, O families of nations, ascribe to the LORD glory and strength.* [8] *Ascribe to the LORD the glory due his name; bring an offering and come into his courts.* [9] *Worship the LORD in the splendor of his holiness; tremble before him, all the earth.* [10] *Say among the nations, "The LORD reigns." The world is firmly established, it cannot be moved; he will judge the peoples with equity.*

From self-government to civil government, we must submit to Christ's authority.

Any nation that takes God out of the equation will perish. The prophet Isaiah warns us of this in Isaiah 60:12 (NIV) *[12] For the nation or kingdom that will not serve you will perish; it will be utterly ruined.*

Every nation that has turned away from God has the opportunity to repent and turn to God for mercy. *Jeremiah 18:7-10 (NIV) [7] If at any time I announce that a nation or kingdom is to be uprooted, torn down and destroyed, [8] and if that nation I warned repents of its evil, then I will relent and not inflict on it the disaster I had planned. [9] And if at another time I announce that a nation or kingdom is to be built up and planted, [10] and if it does evil in my sight and does not obey me, then I will reconsider the good I had intended to do for it.*

It is in the name of Jesus that our nation must put its trust. The Bible says in Matthew 12:18-21 (NIV)[18] "Here is my servant whom I have chosen, the one I love, in whom I delight; I will put my Spirit on him, and he will proclaim justice to the nations...[21] In his name the nations will put their hope."

When God was blessing Abraham, He was thinking about the nation of America. *Galatians 3:8-9 (NIV) [8] The Scripture foresaw that God would justify the Gentiles by faith, and announced the gospel in advance to Abraham:* **"All nations** *will be blessed through you." [9] So those who have faith are blessed along with*

Abraham, the man of faith. America is a nation that was built on faith in Jesus; and America has been blessed. But if we do not repent and return to making Christ our Lord, America will be one of the prophesied nations that will be destroyed.

Where do we go from here? We must admit that we have been coveting earthly things and earthly comforts. We have been discontent with what the Lord has provided for us and we have allowed our hearts to covet the things of this world. We have been so focused upon what we want that we have allowed Jesus to be taken out of our homes, schools, courthouses, and the very government that is supposed to be protecting us.

We can no longer hide and be ashamed of our faith; for our faith in Jesus is the very thing that can save this nation. Be bold, be brave, be men and women of courage! Be unashamed of who Jesus is and what He has done for you.

I am not ashamed of the gospel in the public school, in city hall, at the courthouse, in the White House, in my neighborhood, and especially in my home. The gospel is what will transform our nation, but we must submit to Jesus as our Lord. We must set our hearts upon Jesus and know His Word. *Psalm 111:10 (NIV)* *[10] The fear of the LORD is the beginning of wisdom; all who follow his precepts have good understanding. To him belongs eternal praise.*

Proverbs 9:10 (NIV) [10] *"The fear of the LORD is the beginning of wisdom, and knowledge of the Holy One is understanding.* We must covet after God and His Word to understand the fear of the Lord. We must memorize God's Word and cry out to God for wisdom.

Proverbs 2:1-7 (NIV) [1] *My son, if you accept my words and store up my commands within you,* [2] *turning your ear to wisdom and applying your heart to understanding,* [3] *and if you call out for insight and cry aloud for understanding,* [4] *and if you look for it as for silver and search for it as for hidden treasure,* [5] *then you will understand the fear of the LORD and find the knowledge of God.* [6] *For the LORD gives wisdom, and from his mouth come knowledge and understanding.* [7] *He holds victory in store for the upright, he is a shield to those whose walk is blameless,*

We need to return to the days when the Bible was the main textbook in our lives, in our homes, and in our schools. God's biblical institutions remain the building blocks for a free society today.

WE ARE RETURNING TO AND <u>NOT</u> ESTABLISHING NEW

To some people it seems radical and new to speak about making Jesus the Lord of our nation and to use His Word as the source for our laws. But it is not radical and new. It is returning to what our founders established in the early days of this nation.

The Mayflower Compact written by William Bradford states, "Having undertaken, for the Glory of God, and advancements of the Christian faith, and the honor of our King and Country, a voyage to plant the first colony in the Northern parts of Virginia; do by these presents, solemnly and mutually, in the presence of God, and one another, covenant and combine ourselves together into a civil body politic."

The Mayflower Compact was their way of fulfilling the Great Commission. *Matthew 28:18-20 (NIV)* [18] *Then Jesus came to them and said, "All authority in heaven and on earth has been given to me.* [19] *Therefore go and make disciples of all nations, baptizing them in the name of the Father and of the Son and of the Holy Spirit,* [20] *and teaching them to obey everything I have commanded you. And surely I am with you always, to the very end of the age."*

Believers have a responsibility to proclaim Christ to the nations and seek to teach them the ways of God. The responsibility begins individually, then in our families, our churches, and our nation. Paul wrote these closing remarks in a letter to the Romans in *Romans 16:25-27 (NIV)* [25] *Now to him who is able to establish you by my gospel and the proclamation of Jesus Christ, according to the revelation of the mystery hidden for long ages past,* [26] *but now revealed and made known through the prophetic writings by the command of the eternal God,* **so that all nations might believe and obey him—** [27] *to the only wise God be glory forever through Jesus Christ! Amen.*

With this mindset our founders wrote the Declaration of Independence which states, "We hold these truths to be self-evident, that all men are created equal, that they are endowed by their Creator with certain unalienable Rights, that among these are Life, Liberty and the pursuit of Happiness. — That to secure these rights, Governments are instituted among Men, deriving their just powers from the consent of the governed."

The government should derive their just powers from the consent of the governed. To do this we must **covet** the things of God and be intent upon building God's kingdom here upon the earth.

Matthew 6:9-10 (NIV) [9] "This, then, is how you should pray: "'Our Father in heaven, hallowed be your name, [10] **your kingdom come, your will be done on earth** as it is in heaven."

Matthew 5:6 (NIV) [6] Blessed are those who hunger and thirst for righteousness, for they will be filled.

Thomas Jefferson said, "Can the liberties of a nation be thought secure when we have removed their only firm basis, a conviction… that these liberties are the gift of God."

John Adams said, "It is religion and morality alone, which can establish the principles upon which freedom can securely stand."

Do you believe that we should have prayer in our public schools?

Do you believe that we should be using the Bible as the primary textbook in our schools?

Do you believe that we should seek to live by the Ten Commandments and the teachings of Christ?

Do you believe that our leaders should use the Scriptures as our source of law when they govern society and write the laws for society? Or should they just put their hand upon the Bible when they are sworn in?

These are not new ideas or principles for our nation. This is what the consent of the governed believed and established. This is what I believe and desire for our nation. This is how I will vote and speak up within our nation. I will govern my life by God's four biblical institutions. I will do my best to evangelize and teach others why God's principles are best.

What about you? When your life is over, what will they say about you? Will they say that you did all that you could to bring God's kingdom here upon the earth? Will they say that you were instrumental in changing your community for Christ? Or will they say that you kept to yourself; coveting the things of this world? Will they say you sat quietly and watched the nation crumble?

GO! Make disciples of all nations, teaching them to obey all things.

WORKSHEET FOR CIVIL GOVERNMENT
LIFE TRUTH # 10
YOU SHALL NOT COVET

Question: What does it mean to covet?
Answer: Coveting is setting our hearts on earthly things instead of on heavenly things.

Exodus 20:17 (NIV) [17] *"You shall not covet your neighbor's house. You shall not covet your neighbor's wife, or his manservant or maidservant, his ox or donkey, or anything that belongs to your neighbor."*

> Write out the Life Truth, question, and answer on one side of an index card and the verse on the other side. Keep it in your Bible for the week. Work on it every day individually and as a family. Have it memorized by next week.

Read Joshua, Chapter 7. Why couldn't Israel defeat their enemies?

What did Achan covet?

Why is coveting dangerous?

Read Luke 12:13-34. What did Jesus mean when he said, "A man's life does not consist in the abundance of his possessions?"

Instead of focusing on "taking life easy" what should a person be focusing upon?

Being content means being satisfied with what the Lord provides for us. How is coveting related to not being content?

Put in your own words the meaning of this phrase, *"For where your treasure is, there your heart will be also."* What kinds of things do we need to be careful to not set our hearts upon?

Read Colossians 3:1-4. What does it mean to set our hearts and minds on things above?

In what ways does our generation encourage us to covet?

Entitlement is a form of coveting. (It is my right to have). Does God owe us anything? Why or why not?

Do we owe God anything? Why or why not? (1 Cor. 6:19-20)

Why is coveting such a dangerous vice to society?

What can we do to help our hearts stay focused on "things above" instead of on earthly things?

Based on this LIFE TRUTH, are there things that you are coveting now? How can you help others understand more about the seriousness of coveting?